Knitted Wire Jewelry

Jewelry

Techniques Projects Inspiration

SAMANTHA A. LOPEZ

NORTH LIGHT BOOKS
Cincinnati, Ohio

www.mycraftivity.com

Other fine North Light titles are available from your local bookstore, craft supply store, online retailer or visit our website at www.fwmedia.com.

13 12 11 10 09   5 4 3 2 1

Distributed in Canada by Fraser Direct
100 Armstrong Avenue
Georgetown, ON, Canada L7G 5S4
Tel: (905) 877-4411

Distributed in the U.K. and Europe by David & Charles
Brunel House, Newton Abbot, Devon, TQ12 4PU, England
Tel: (+44) 1626 323200, Fax: (+44) 1626 323319
Email: postmaster@davidandcharles.co.uk

Distributed in Australia by Capricorn Link
P.O. Box 704, S. Windsor, NSW 2756 Australia
Tel: (02) 4577-3555

Editor: JESSICA STRAWSER
Production Editor: LIZ CASLER
Designer: KELLY O'DELL
Photographers: CHRISTINE POLOMSKY, AL PARRISH, RIC DELIANTONI
Production Coordinator: GREG NOCK
Stylist: NORA MARTINI

Library of Congress Cataloging-in-Publication Data
Lopez, Samantha.
   Knitted wire jewelry : techniques, projects, inspiration / Samantha Lopez. – 1st ed.
       p. cm.
   Includes index.
   ISBN 978-1-60061-157-5 (pbk.)
   1. Jewelry making. 2. Knitting–Patterns. 3. Wire craft. I. Title.
   TT212.L665 2009
   745.594'2–dc22
                        2008047778

www.fwmedia.com

Metric Conversion Chart		
to convert	**to**	**multiply by**
Inches	Centimeters	2.54
Centimeters	Inches	0.4
Feet	Centimeters	30.5
Centimeters	Feet	0.03
Yards	Meters	0.9
Meters	Yards	1.1
Sq. Inches	Sq. Centimeters	6.45
Sq. Centimeters	Sq. Inches	0.16
Sq. Feet	Sq. Meters	0.09
Sq. Meters	Sq. Feet	10.8
Sq. Yards	Sq. Meters	0.8
Sq. Meters	Sq. Yards	1.2
Pounds	Kilograms	0.45
Kilograms	Pounds	2.2
Ounces	Grams	28.3
Grams	Ounces	0.035

DEDICATION & ACKNOWLEDGMENTS

Dedication

To my husband, Richard: Without your love, trust, commitment and support, none of this would have been possible. Thank you.

Acknowledgments

I would first like to thank my mother, Susana, whose unconditional love and support has given me the courage to do anything. I would also like to thank my dad, Renato Sr., and my brothers, Renato and Arturo, who always let me think everything I did was wonderful. To the rest of my family: Bob, Moira, Harold, Missy, Edward, Linda, Claudio, Tiana, Sebastian and Denise, thank you. And finally, to Nani, I know you would have loved to see what I did with the knitting skills you taught me. I love you all.

Thanks also to the team at F+W: To Jessica Strawser, whose hard work has made this all seem easy; Christine Polomsky, the amazing photographer who somehow knew exactly how to capture the tiniest of details; and finally, to Suzanne Lucas, for somehow finding my work, and to Tonia Davenport, for believing in it.

About the Author

Samantha A. Lopez was born in Mexico City but spent most of her time as a child in the countryside of the state of Morelos. She moved to New York City to study at Pratt Institute School of Art and Design, where she received her degree in fine art with a concentration in sculpture. Her work has been exhibited at the Rubelle and Norman Schafler Gallery and Object Image Gallery in Brooklyn, New York.

The Knotstudio line of jewelry can be found online at *www.knotstudio.com* as well as in select boutiques in the New York City area.

Contents

INTRODUCTION

This was all my husband's idea. He was not my husband then; we were both in art school, and I was incredibly poor and frustrated because I wanted to make a big, metal sculpture (I am a small woman, and, yes, I probably have a Napoleon complex) but had very little money to spend on materials, so I was trying to figure out a way to make a mesh to cover the surfaces by welding lots of steel rods. That's when he suggested I just knit it. It was kind of a joke—I had just learned how to knit and was knitting hideous sweaters for him and myself on an addictive level, which is probably why he suggested I put my energy into a different project—but I took him seriously, and the next thing I knew, I was knitting bare copper speaker wire into a gigantic kinetic sculpture.

After graduating from art school, I lost my studio, but I was still fascinated by the idea that, through knitting, I could transform a cold, hard material into a soft, organic fabric, so I kept experimenting, but this time with smaller needles and thinner, silver wire. One day I put two of those pieces onto some ear wires, and soon my friends and family began pushing me to make more. So I launched Knotstudio as a side project. After having worked for a designer in the jewelry industry for some time, I decided to quit and dedicate all my efforts to the project.

6

Because of my Mexican background, I always had a hard time with the terms art and craft because, in Spanish, there is a word that in a way bridges both—*artesania*—which is a traditional craft so special it is considered a work of art. So, even though I had been trained as a sculptor and had been using materials and tools to make artwork, I was also knitting and making jewelry, which in many worlds are considered crafts. I had no idea how to make money doing this until, eventually, trends shifted and both boutique and art gallery owners began to take an interest.

Although at first the projects in this book may seem complicated and even intimidating, they are all made up of several very basic and accessible techniques, all of which are explained in detail. Anyone can learn how to knit, string beads or loop wire, but it is the application of all these techniques into one piece of jewelry that makes the work unique.

The most important thing to keep in mind is the medium. Because the processes discussed in the book bridge several techniques, the materials used for each also change. These material differences are not obstacles but opportunities for innovation. For instance, metal wire, whether it is copper, silver or gold, is fundamentally different than a fiber yarn and therefore will behave differently when knit. A wire panel will not drape the same way a fiber one would but instead remains stiff. Yet this fact also allows this same wire panel to be curled and folded into shapes that hold up, making it possible to explore new boundaries.

Even though no prior skills are required to make any of the projects in the book, I wanted to make sure people with experience in either knitting or jewelry making, but not necessarily both, could approach them. Therefore I designed them so that anyone could be comfortable trying something new. Even if you have no experience with either craft, you should find everything you need to know on the following pages. Some of the twenty-five projects in this book are simpler than others, but the more complicated ones are not difficult; they are just more time consuming. All offer an opportunity for discovery.

MATERIALS

Having started out as a sculptor, my arsenal of tools and materials was more that of a construction worker than that of a fine jeweler. But, with a few modifications, I was able to work with what I had. With time, and as I became more acquainted with the jewelry world, I began to acquire tools as I needed them and started to work with finer materials. But I still have a few tools I cannot get out of the habit of using, and the freedom that comes from working with nonprecious materials can sometimes produce some fantastically unexpected pieces.

It is in that spirit—understanding that everyone's budget and access to materials will be different—that the pieces for this book were designed. Although most of the projects are made with sterling silver, this is by no means a requirement. Any of the projects can be made from a huge range of materials, from inexpensive craft wire (or even deconstructed speaker wire, which I used when I got started) to precious metals such as silver and gold. Some are easier to find than others, but most can be found at local craft and hardware stores. It's up to you to determine how basic or elaborate you want to get with the projects.

BASIC JEWELRY MATERIALS

Although the processes discussed in the book are not exactly conventional to jewelry making, the materials remain basic.

Wire

The main property to consider when choosing wire is the metal's malleability, or ability to adapt to being shaped or formed without cracking or breaking. Although inexpensive wires, such as colored copper craft wire, are available in only one degree of hardness (soft), finer silver and gold wires are available in a wide range (dead soft, soft, half hard and hard). Because knitting requires the metal to bend repeatedly, a soft (for the sake of your hands) and malleable wire, unless specified otherwise or unless the wire is being used to support a structure (e.g. hoop earrings), is the best choice.

The gauge, or thickness, of the wire is also a major influence. The standard wire gauge system used in the United States is the American wire gauge, or Brown & Sharpe wire gauge, and the general rule to keep in mind is that as the gauge number increases, the diameter of the wire decreases. Basically this is because when wire is made or drawn, the thinner you want the wire, the more times it must be drawn. Thinner wire is easier to bend and form, especially with small needles, so wire between 28- and 30-gauge is preferred.

Metal wire is available in many different shapes, from round, half round (flat on one side) and square to triangular tubes. Although there are a few projects in the book that specify using half-round wires, round is the general shape of the wires used throughout.

When purchasing wire, look for the specifications in shape, thicknesses or gauges, alloys and degrees of hardness. For instance, 30-gauge fine silver round wire, dead soft, means the shape of the wire is round; its thickness is 30-gauge, or .255mm (.01") in diameter; its alloy (the combination of metals that make up the wire; for instance, sterling silver is 92.5 percent pure silver and 7.5 percent copper, while Argentium sterling silver is silver with germanium as the copper replacement), fine silver, is 99.9 percent pure silver; and its hardness is dead soft, which is perfect for bending. I prefer sterling silver or Argentium sterling silver: The Argentium in particular is quite resistant to discoloration. Fine silver wire is incredibly easy to use due to its softness, but it tarnishes rather quickly, so I prefer to reserve it for projects that incorporate a patina.

Sheet Metal

Metal that has been rolled into sheets is probably one of the most versatile forms of the material, as it can be easily transformed. Precious metals such as silver and gold are the ones most commonly seen in jewelry, but there are many different kinds of metals that can be made into sheets. Like wire, it is offered in gauges, and, as such, the larger the number, the thinner the sheet. Sheet metal is usually sold in pieces precut to certain dimensions (e.g. 2" wide × 6" long [5cm × 15cm]), so if you plan to make more than one

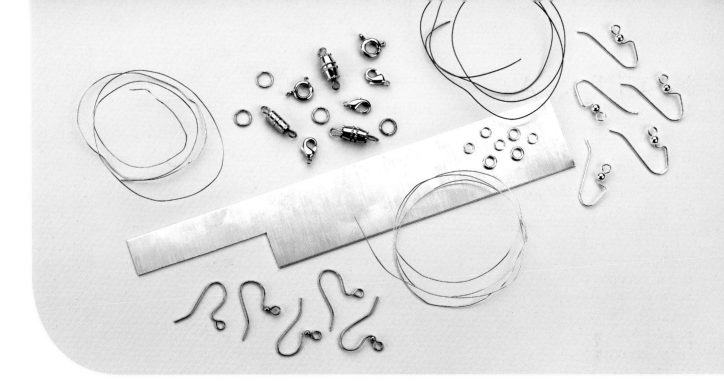

project that uses sheet metal, add together the dimensions of each piece used and make sure the sheet you purchase can accommodate them all. All the pieces in the book require 22-gauge sheet metal to make this process easier (and sterling silver is my sheet metal of choice).

Findings

I started out making and therefore soldering most of my findings, but prefabricated findings are now relatively inexpensive and easy to locate. Keeping that in mind, I designed the patterns so that the need to make and solder findings for any of the projects can be eliminated. However, if you choose to make your own, most of the projects specify the materials you would need to make them. Again, although all findings shown are Argentium or sterling silver, as long as you stay within the measurements, you can use whatever materials you wish.

EAR WIRES

Earring shapes vary greatly, but throughout the book, I prefer to use simple French ear wires, as their shape is elegant and muted, letting the work shine through. These can be purchased with their loops open or soldered closed (closed are a bit harder to find but offer a more secure construction). If you prefer to make your own, like I do, note that the handmade French ear wires shown throughout this book are made of 21- or 22-gauge wire and measure approximately 1" (2.5cm) long by ⅖" (1cm) wide.

CLASPS

Hook clasps are graceful and easy to use, particularly when used in bracelets. These, too, can be store bought, but to replicate the handmade hook clasps shown throughout this book, you'll need 18- to 23-gauge Argentium or sterling silver wire about 8mm–10mm (.31"–.4") long to make a hook about 4.4mm–5mm (.173"–.2") wide.

JUMP RINGS

Simple rings used to connect parts of the jewelry pieces (such as clasps) can be made by coiling wire, but are also readily available premade through jewelry suppliers. They are available split open or soldered closed as well as in a variety of gauges and sizes. I prefer to purchase them closed, as they can be knit or looped into place without compromising safety. Throughout the book, the three most widely used sizes are:

* 18-gauge Argentium or sterling silver jump ring, soldered closed (5mm) (.2")

* 23-gauge Argentium or sterling silver jump ring soldered closed (4mm) (.16")

9

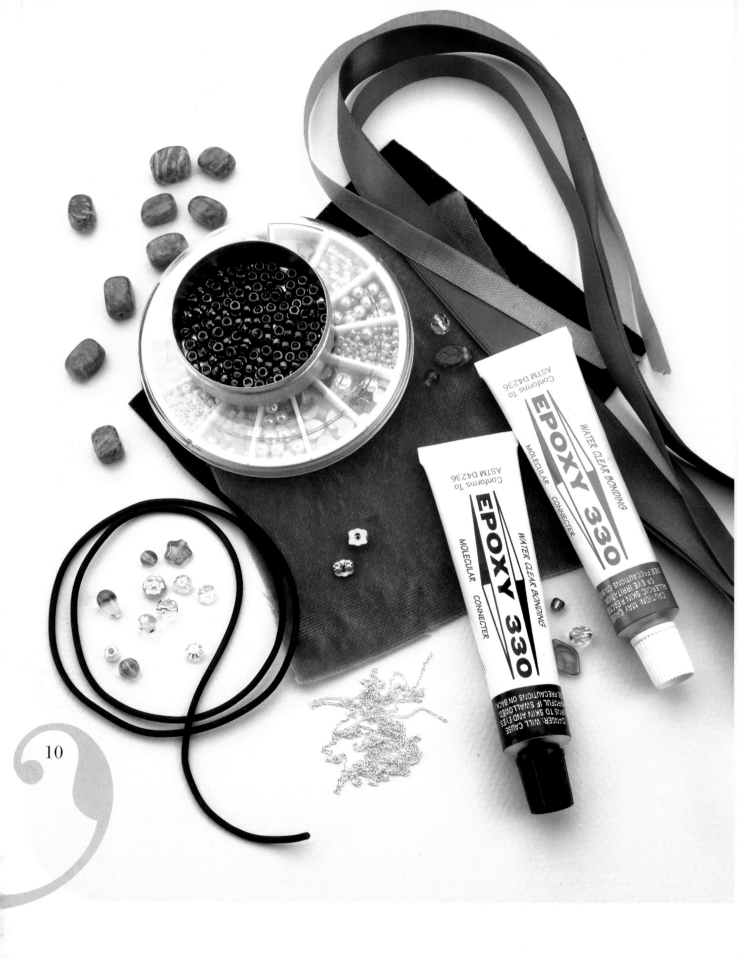

* 21-gauge Argentium or sterling silver jump ring, soldered closed (5mm) (.2")

POSTS AND EAR NUTS

Although earrings using posts and nuts are popular, in this book they are used in only the *Small Hoops* (project on page 60). As opposed to the French wires, posts keep the earrings close to the earlobe, a quality that was useful when designing the *Hoops*. Both components (the posts and the ear nuts) are available commercially and although the posts can easily be made from wire, the nuts are much more difficult.

* Ear nuts .72" × .4" (18.4mm × 10mm) that fit post diameters .026"–.036" (.66mm–.91mm)
* Posts 1.5" (4cm) long and with the wire diameter of .026"–.036" (.66mm–.91mm)

Chain

Jewelry chain is an extremely versatile product as it can be used not only for necklaces, but also as a component of smaller pieces, such as the *Gradient Drop Earrings* (page 68) and the *Coral Bracelet* (page 80). In keeping with the delicate look of the knitting, I stick to very tiny, basic styles. In all, chain adds a flowing dangly effect.

* 1mm (.04") Argentium or sterling silver round cable chain
* 1.75mm (.07") Argentium or sterling silver round cable chain

Ribbon, Fabric and Rubber Cord

Pairing knitted metal with fabrics known for their softness makes an interesting contrast. Silk satin ribbons and velvets are two of my favorite materials, though you can substitute less expensive ones of your choice.

Rubber cord is a versatile material that can appear both industrial and polished. It tends to last longer than leather and does not fray like the cotton substitutes. (All the rubber cord shown in this book is 2mm [.08"].)

Beads

In my work, I regularly use natural gemstone beads in keeping with the organic aesthetic I strive to achieve. I try not to overpower the knit work with beads, but instead use smaller beads to complement the designs. The beads used here have a broad range in price (which has also been shown to fluctuate according to supply and demand), but most now have synthetic alternatives at a fraction of the cost, so feel free to substitute them as you need.

My preferences for the shapes of the beads I use vary with the particular shape and feel of the project. Some varieties come with a hole drilled at the top from side to side (top-drilled), such as the round, faceted (or cut all around) teardrops; pear-cut briolettes (pear-shaped teardrops that are not fully rounded but slightly flat); table, or taviz-cut, briolettes (rounder and shorter than a teardrop); and smooth teardrops (not faceted but simply polished). Top-drilled beads are great for dangling. Faceted rounds and rondelles (rondelles are a little flatter than the round) are good for using in clusters. Round beads that are also side-drilled and a little flat—but with little or no faceting—are called abacus (a bit flatter), or button. These can often be found in strands of graduated color, as is the case with tourmaline.

Irregular shapes can be the cheapest but also the most organic and interesting. Chips or pebbles of turquoise highlight the many different hues of the stone, and coral branches add bold shapes to simple contours.

Lastly, freshwater pearls are inexpensive and are now being dyed into some incredible colors. Though they can come in a variety of shapes, such as coin, stick, potato and even cross, my favorites are still the well-known rice-shaped ones.

Adhesives and Enamels

Adhesives such as clear epoxies or jewelers' cements are used to secure any loose ends that remain after trimming excess wire. The ends are tucked into the work, and a very small bead of epoxy or cement is placed in the end with a toothpick. Whether you choose to use an epoxy or a jewelers' cement, the two most important things to keep in mind are that it dries clear (most products indicate this on the packaging) and that it bonds metals.

To keep ribbons and other textiles from fraying, gently brush the cut edges with clear nail polish. Any brand, as long as it dries clear, can be used for these purposes.

TOOLS

JEWELRY-MAKING TOOLS

Due to the fact that the word *jewelry* covers a wide range of styles, materials and methods, the tools necessary to make the jewelry differ dramatically with the processes. A person working with mostly beads will need a completely different set of tools than someone who works entirely by casting metals. Because the process of knitting wire combines several techniques, the tools needed also vary.

Jeweler's Saw and Blades

A jeweler's saw looks like a petite version of a coping saw, with a C-shaped frame and easily removable blades. The blades come in a range of standardized sizes (the size corresponds to the number of teeth per inch, and more teeth generally means a finer blade), and most manufacturers have charts that recommend the correct blade size for the particular size of the metal you are cutting (I use a size 4 for a lot of my work).

Pliers and Cutters

There are pliers for every specialty in the jewelry world, but for the purposes of this book, you will need only two kinds: a pair of needle-nose (or round-nose) pliers for forming wire and a pair of Nylon-covered coiling flat jaw pliers. The latter looks similar to the needle-nose, except that one of the jaws is flat and covered in Nylon to protect the wire, while the other jaw remains round.

A pair of wire cutters is also necessary, and there are again several kinds. The most common are side cutters (which have the cutting blades on the side, like scissors, and fine tips) and end cutters (which have the cutting blades on the top in order to cut close to the objects). Uses for both can be found throughout the book, but use what you can find and afford.

Tweezers

Tweezers are an invaluable tool when working with such small parts and wires, so a sturdy fine-pointed metal pair (or two) allows even the clumsiest of fingers to handle fine work. They are readily available at most jewelry suppliers as well as some craft stores. As a rule, the finer the point, the better, but they are available in many lengths, so purchase whatever is most comfortable in your hands.

Needle Files

Needle files come in many different shapes, but there are relatively inexpensive sets available that contain the most basic files (round, flat, half round and square).

Ruler and Straightedge

A straightedged ruler is especially useful if it is marked with smaller increments (1⁄32" or millimeters if metric) for ease in precise measuring.

12

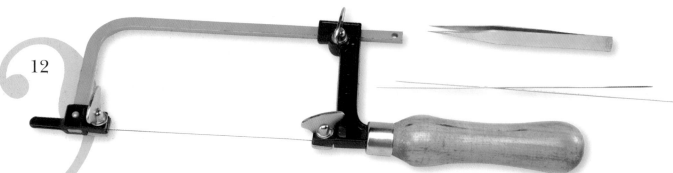

Clockwise from left: A jeweler's saw; a pair of size AA fine-pointed tweezers; size US 0000 (1.25mm) knitting needles.

Clockwise from bottom: A jeweler's
hand drill; a set of assorted drill
bits; a rubber mallet.

Awl

An awl is a pointed metal spike useful for marking metal before drilling or cutting.

Drilling

Jeweler's hand drills are available in most jewelry supply or other hobby and craft stores and should have an adjustable chuck to hold bits of different sizes. The bits are sold separately or in sets. The bits are much smaller than those of an ordinary hand drill, and range in sizes from no. 61 to no. 80.

Hammering

Similar to a hammer, a mallet differs in that the head of a mallet is usually made of softer materials—such as rubber, rawhide or nylon—to avoid damaging the surface of the metal.

Ring Mandrel

Used for forming rings, these are available commercially and have marks for ring sizes on them. Use this in conjunction with the ring sizing charts on page 15 for accurate sizing.

KNITTED JEWELRY TOOLS

Tools that are specific to the process of knitting wire are not generally available, so a combination of tools found in hardware, craft, jewelry and knitting supply stores are listed below. Some, such as the drawplate, can be made at home.

Needles

Because knitting needles are such a basic tool, they can be constructed if not easily found. Knitting wire for the projects in this book requires size U.S. 0000 (1.25mm) metal straight knitting needles (see *Resources*, page 126, for information on where I get mine). Although no other tools provide the flexibility of knitting needles, you can make your own in a pinch, as I initially did, out of thin steel rods attached to dowel rods for handles (all found at a local hardware store). You can also use soldering picks: Simply file down the points. (As a bonus, both of these options do offer more comfortable handles than do the needles.) For projects that require cabling, like the *Patinated Silver Cable Cuff* on page 92, you'll also need a small safety pin on hand to use as a cable needle.

Clamps

The projects in the book that feature Viking knitting will require the use of two kinds of clamps or fasteners—a C-clamp and a vise grip. The shape of a C-clamp allows the frame to go around objects, such as tables, and they have adjustable pins. Vise grips are also adjustable but resemble pliers. They are useful in that they can release their hold easily. Both can also be used to secure sheet metal while it is being cut, but be sure to use a protective surface such as wood or fabric to avoid marking the metal with the clamps. Protective surfaces can be found at most hardware stores.

13

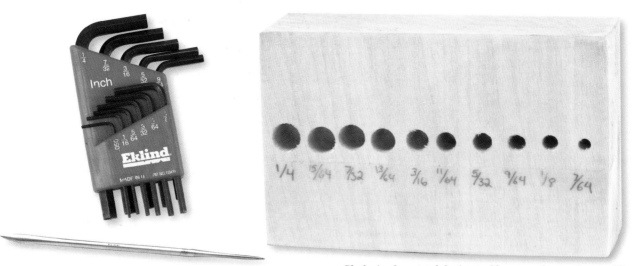

Clockwise from top left: A set of hexagonal wrenches, or Allen keys, in assorted sizes; a simple homemade wooden drawplate labeled with the size of each hole; a metal burnisher.

Hexagonal (Hex) Wrenches or Allen Keys

Used for the Viking knitting projects (see pages 24–26), these wrenches come in sets but can also be purchased individually. They are also available at most hardware stores. The projects in this book use hexagonal wrenches in the following sizes: 7/64" (2.8mm), 1/8" (3.2mm), 9/64" (3.6mm), 5/32" (4mm), 3/16" (4.8mm), 13/64" (5.2mm), 7/32" (5.6mm) and 1/4" (6.4mm).

Wooden Drawplate

Basically, this is just a piece of wood with drilled holes that are marked. As you pull Viking knitting through the holes, the drawplate essentially compacts the work, resulting in more uniformity in the stitches. Drawplates are available commercially through jewelry and craft stores, but you can make your own out of a scrap piece of wood and, for the projects in this book, with drill bits ranging from 1/4" (6.4m) down to 7/64" (2.8mm) (1/4" [6.4mm], 15/64" [6mm], 7/32" [5.6mm], etc.).

TEXTURING, POLISHING AND BURNISHING TOOLS

Abrasives

Several kinds and grades of abrasives are useful in not only texturing the metal but also in preparing the surface to be polished. Common household scouring pads (such as Brillo, Scotch-Brite, etc.) are excellent for removing stray tool marks and serve to even out the surface with a texture. Sandpaper is available in many grades based on the size of the grit, but for the projects in this book, use only fine to very fine grit (finishing) sandpaper or a sanding pad (I use a 30/40-micron, or about 340/280 grit, double-sided sanding pad). Steel wool, also in very fine grades (000–0000) is used as a tool to texture and polish.

Polishing

After the surface has been prepared with very fine abrasives, a polishing cloth and polishing compounds, such as jeweler's rouge and white rouge, give the surface a bright, shiny finish. You can find both products separately, but there are some polishing cloths that come impregnated with different compounds.

Burnishing

A steel burnisher is a basic, curved tool, usually made of metal, used to remove marks and to polish by rubbing. It is useful for a variety of applications and because of this, they can be found at most art, craft and jewelry supply stores.

Patina Supplies

Liver of sulfur has been traditionally used to darken the surface of metals such as silver and bronze. It is available in powder, lump and liquid (already diluted) forms. I prefer to use it in lump form because it lasts longer and I can dilute it to make it as weak or as strong as I like. It is toxic, so basic precautions, such as securing adequate ventilation, should be taken. Although the process is much slower and messier, egg yolks can also be used to darken silver. So, if you can't find liver of sulfur, you can always boil an egg and place it—along with the object to be darkened—inside a sealed plastic bag, and crush it. The sulfur in the egg will slowly color the metal. You'll want to have paper towels and scraps of cardboard on hand as well when working with patina supplies.

Waxes are used to seal the patina on the metal and, in some cases, to mask areas not meant to be darkened.

Butcher's wax, paint wax or cold wax painting medium will suffice. You'll also want to have paintbrushes on hand to apply the wax:

* Fine-tip soft artist's brushes (size 2/0 or smaller) to accurately apply the wax and patina (especially useful in the *Etched Striped Ring* [page 48] where the lines are so tiny).

* Small, very soft brush (cheap makeup brushes work well) to brush wax over an already patinated piece without marking it.

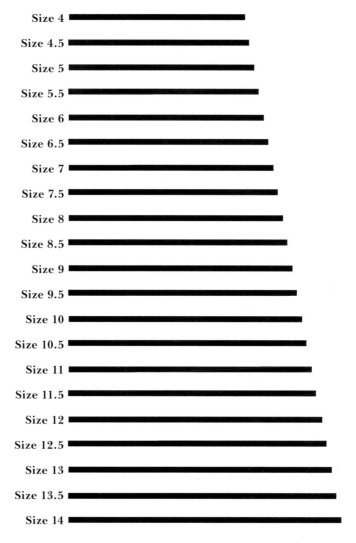

Ring-sizing charts shown at actual size. Above: length of sheet metal needed for bands in common ring sizes Below: diameters of common ring sizes.

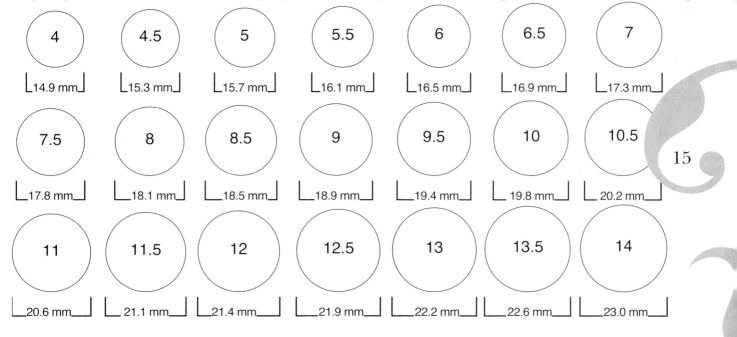

15

1 PART ONE
techniques

All the techniques you need to know to make the projects are covered in this section of the book. First you'll learn the basic knitting techniques most commonly used with fibers and you'll discover the difference that changing the medium makes on the process. A variation of circular knitting is also covered. At first glance, knitting wire with such tiny needles may seem overwhelmingly time-consuming and mechanical, but, once working on the piece, you will discover a sense of rhythm and focus from this very repetition that is incredibly meditative.

Because you also need to have an understanding of some basic jewelry-making processes, I've included a clear introduction to them here. While some techniques are essential to any kind of jewelry making, others are adapted specifically for knitted wire.

Finally, you'll encounter a process unique to working with metal, the use of a patina, and you'll learn the many ways to use its properties.

As you complete the projects, you'll notice that the instructions sometimes cross-reference the individual techniques used for their assembly. Use the following pages as a guide and come back to review the processes if you ever feel uncertain.

TECHNIQUES FOR BASIC KNITTING

Knitting, the process by which a fabric is made by looping a fiber, can be easily adapted for other materials. On the following pages you will learn, step by step, the basic knitting techniques used in the projects in this book. If you do not already know how to knit, this will teach you everything you need to know. If you already have experience knitting with fiber, you may still want to look through this section: It's helpful to note up front the differences in tension that come with knitting metal wires.

Casting On

In knitting, "casting on" describes the process of making the first stitches that will become the foundation for the project. While there are several methods for casting on, all the projects in the book use the long-tail cast-on demonstrated here.

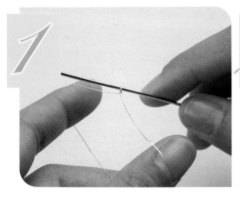

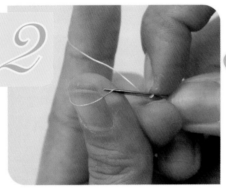

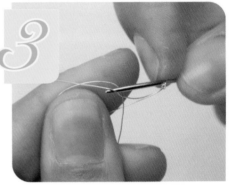

Step 1: Tie slipknot
Tie a slipknot in the wire, leaving a sufficient tail (I leave a tail of 4"–5" [10cm–13cm] to cast on 22 stitches), depending on how many stitches you are casting on. Position the knot a few inches from the tip of your knitting needles and pull it snug. Wrap the tail around your thumb and the working end around your index finger of your left hand.

Step 2: Insert needle into tail
Holding the slipknot in place with your right hand, slide the tip of the needle into the loop of wire wrapped around your thumb, as shown.

Step 3: Wrap the other wire end
Keeping the needle inside the wire loop you picked up in step 2, hook it behind the wire wrapped around your index finger, as well.

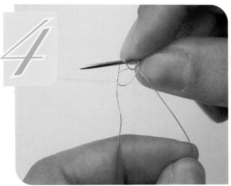

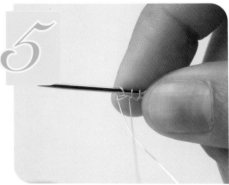

Step 4: Draw back strand through front loop
Begin gently pulling the wire end that you hooked in step 3 through the thumb loop to create a second, loose loop on your needle that will be the cast-on stitch. Gently pull the wire ends to tighten.

Step 5: Tighten stitch and repeat
Repeat steps 2–4 to cast on the desired number of stitches necessary for your pattern. Include the slipknot in your stitch count.

Knitting

Along with the purl stitch, the knit stitch is the most basic element in knitting. Although simple, both stitches are immensely versatile, and once you learn them both, you will be well on your way to creating knitted wire jewelry (and other types of knitted projects, for that matter!). Combinations and variations of these two stitches make it possible to create all the different stitches and patterns. The two basic methods for both knitting and purling are the English method and the Continental method. You can use either for wire jewelry, but I prefer the former (see instructions below) because it makes the work easier to see—a quality that is very useful with such small wire.

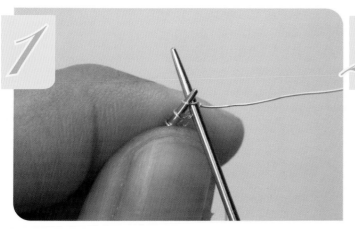

Step 1: Insert needle into first stitch
Insert the right-hand needle into the first stitch on the left-hand needle from front to back, with the right-hand needle crossing behind the left-hand needle.

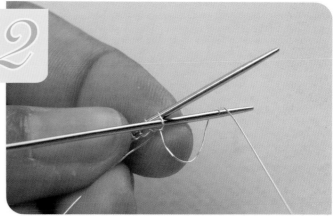

Step 2: Wrap
With your right hand, wrap the working wire around the right-hand needle counterclockwise.

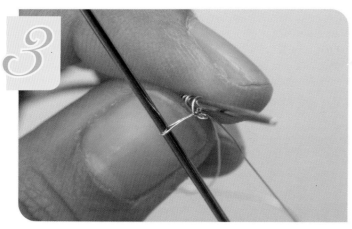

Step 3: Pull loop through stitch
Pull the wrapped wire through the stitch on the left-hand needle.

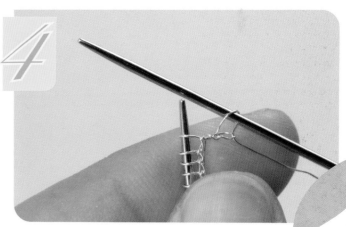

Step 4: Create new stitch
Bring the wire up on the right-hand needle to slide the stitch easily off the left-hand needle and create a new stitch.

Tip — *If you've never knitted with wire (or at all!), practice with inexpensive wire until you get a feel for the process.*

Purling

The purl stitch is the other truly basic knitting stitch and makes up the other half of the Stockinette stitch (see facing page) used throughout the book. It is bumpy in texture and looks like the back of a knit stitch. Because the wire used in these projects is very thin, these bumps look a bit messy (the thickness of yarn would fill in the spaces between stitches, giving them a more uniform look), and therefore the stitch is not usually used on the front of the work. Exceptions to this rule include the *Patinated Silver Cable Cuff* (page 92), where the texture is part of the design, and the beading projects, where the space provided in the purl stitch is large enough to house the bead.

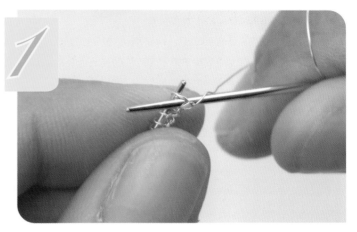

Step 1: Insert needle into first stitch
Insert the right-hand needle into the first stitch on the left-hand needle from back to front, with the right-hand needle crossing in front of the left-hand needle.

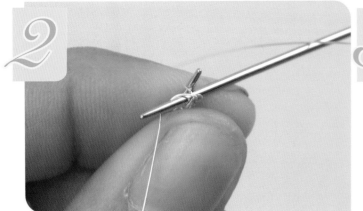

Step 2: Wrap wire around needle
With your right hand, wrap the working wire around the right-hand needle counterclockwise.

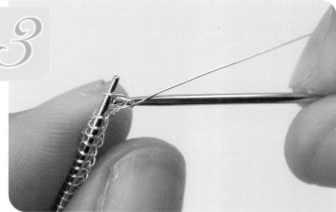

Step 3: Pull loop through stitch
Pull the wrapped wire through the stitch on the left-hand needle.

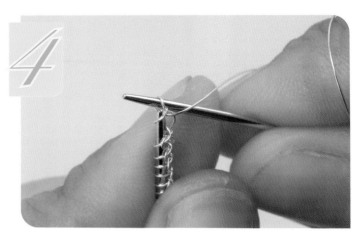

Step 4: Create new stitch
Bring the wire up on the right-hand needle to slide the stitch easily off the left-hand needle and create a new stitch.

Knitting in Stockinette

When you alternate knit and purl rows in a pattern, you are knitting in Stockinette (St st). Except for the *Patinated Silver Cable Cuff* (see page 92) and projects using the Viking knitting technique, almost all the projects in the book use the Stockinette stitch, which has two sides. The smooth side is generally referred to as the "knit side" and is normally the front, and the other bumpy side is the "purl" side and is generally the back. The smooth look of the all-knit side allows for a neater appearance when working with wire. By decreasing or increasing stitches, the shape of the piece can be easily manipulated without overworking the brittle wire and thus avoiding breakage.

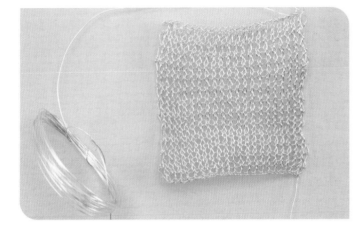

The Stockinette stitch consists of alternating knit and purl rows, which result in a different texture for each side. This square is shown with the knit side as the front; therefore the fabric has a smooth appearance. The back is made up of all purled stitches and is bumpy. This detail shows the cast-on row of 22 stitches at the bottom of the square and the bind-off row at the top.

Increasing

There are many different ways to increase, or add a stitch to a row, but all the projects in this book use one basic increase: knit one front and back (kfb). This is because when working with metal, its malleability, or its ability to be formed without breakage, needs to be taken into consideration, and this method allows the wire to retain its integrity. Metal also "remembers" its shape by taking on marks where bent, so some methods require a lot of twists that would leave unwanted marks. Finally, in all these projects, the increases are done at either the end or beginning of a row, and other methods of increasing require having stitches on either side of the increase.

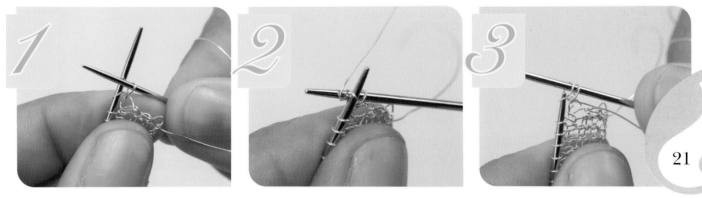

Step 1: Knit into front of stitch
For demonstrative purposes, here I'm starting by casting on 8 stitches and working about 6 rows in Stockinette. To begin the increase at the beginning of a knit row, knit into the front of the first stitch, but don't slip the old stitch off the needle.

Step 2: Knit into back of stitch
Slide the needle in, from top to bottom, through the back of the same stitch you just knit and knit into the back of the stitch.

Step 3: Slide stitch off needle
Slide the stitch off the needle. You now have two loops/stitches instead of one.

Decreasing

To decrease in knitting is to reduce the number of stitches in a given row. There are many different ways to decrease stitches, but all the projects in this book use one basic decrease: knit two together (k2tog). I chose this method because in my designs most of the decreases occur at the edges and other methods require stitches at either end to remain. Decreasing by this method enables you not only to shape the edges, but to ease the stress on the wire, as well.

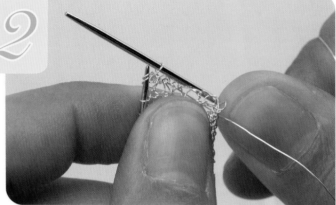

Step 1: Insert needle into first two stitches
Insert the right-hand needle knitwise (from front to back) into the first two stitches on the left-hand needle.

Step 2: Knit stitches together
Knit the two stitches together and slide the new stitch onto the right-hand needle.

Binding Off

Once you have finished knitting the last row in the pattern, you will be left with a row of stitches on the right-hand needle that you will need to fasten, or they will unravel when taken off the needle. This process is called binding off. Binding off can also be used to form the piece—binding off a few stitches in the center of a work will result in a gap, or, if used at the beginning of a row, will change the contour of the edge and act like a more dramatic version of a decrease. Steps 5–6 do not apply to binding off stitches in the middle of a knit piece.

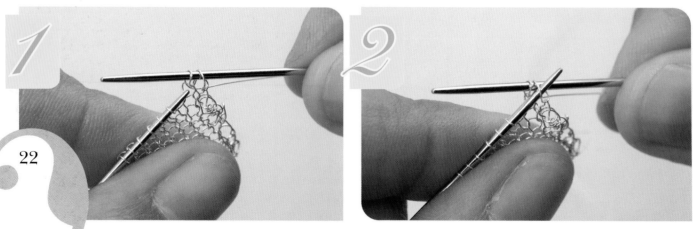

Step 1: Knit the first two stitches loosely
Knit the first two stitches of the row you wish to bind off, resisting the urge to pull them too tight. Looser loops are easier to work with when binding off.

Step 2: Pass first stitch over second stitch
Insert the left-hand needle into the first knitted stitch on the right-hand needle and pass that stitch over the second knitted stitch.

Step 3: Complete bound-off stitch
As you release your left-hand needle from the loop, you'll now have one less stitch on your right-hand needle.

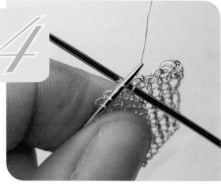

Step 4: Repeat to end of row
Continue binding off stitches in this manner, creating an even bound-off edge, as shown, as you go.

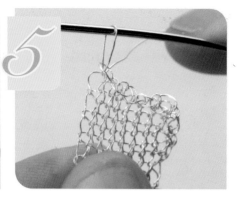

Step 5: Loosen final stitch
When you reach the last stitch, pull the loop loose and remove the needle.

Step 6: Trim and knot end
Trim the end, pass it through the end loop and pull it taut.

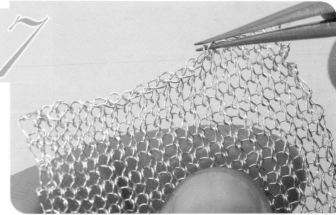

Step 7: Prepare bound-off edge for jewelry
Your bound-off row of stitches will be lying a bit flatly against the last row of your knitting. To create a cleaner edge for your piece of jewelry, use a pair of AA tweezers to lift each loop, one at a time, so they look more like ordinary stitches than a bound-off row.

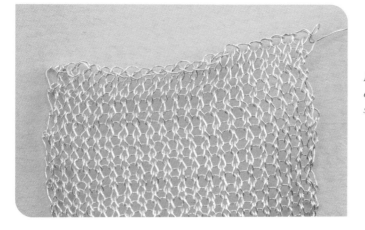

Here you can see more clearly the difference between the lifted bound-off stitches and the others.

23

Creating Viking Knitting

Knitting in the round, or circular knitting, is a technique commonly used to make tubular knit pieces such as sweaters, socks, sleeves, and cords. There are several ways to achieve this, including the use of double-pointed and circular needles, but because it is nearly impossible to get the proper tension in wire, I prefer a variation called Viking knitting for some of the projects. Although the process involves more weaving than it does knitting, the look of the final product is similar to that of I-cord (a thin knitted tube or cord produced by a more common knitting method), but here every stitch has been twisted to resolve the tension issues caused by the wire's stiffness. The result is a smooth chain-like tube that can be easily manipulated into more sculptural forms by adding beads and constricting its circumference. Because this technique leaves no edges, wrapping wire around the ends is not necessary...which makes completing these projects that much easier!

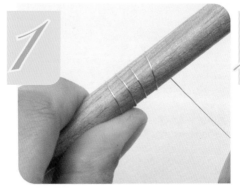 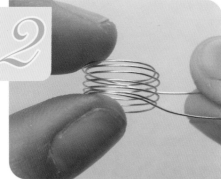 

Step 1: Create spiral
Leave a tail of about 1" (3cm) and wrap the wire 7 times (or however many stitches directed to cast on) around an approximately ⅜" (9.5mm) diameter awl or a dowel rod (the exact size doesn't matter).

Step 2: Slide off rod
Slide the spiral off the rod, push both wire ends to one side and hold, making sure the number of spirals is the same.

Step 3: Pinch loops
Pinch the loops together at the side with the two wire ends.

24

Step 4: Wrap tail
Wrap the tail tightly around all the pinched loop ends.

Step 5: Secure end
Once the smaller tail has been wrapped a few times, thread the remaining length through the small loop openings beneath the wraps to secure.

Step 6: Separate loops
Use the tweezers to separate all the loops and spread them apart like flower petals.

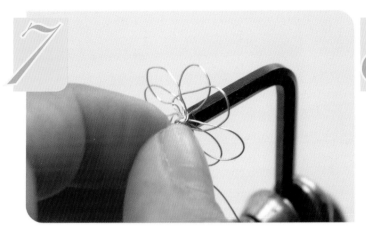

Step 7: Center over hex wrench
Secure a C-clamp to the table with a vise grip. Secure a ⅛"(3.2mm) (or as instructed in the particular pattern) hex wrench in the C-clamp. Face the wrench to the left if you're right-handed and to the right if you're left-handed. Center this wire piece at the end of the wrench.

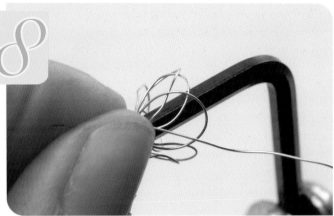

Step 8: Spread loops around hex wrench
Squeeze loops down loosely around the hexagonal wrench.

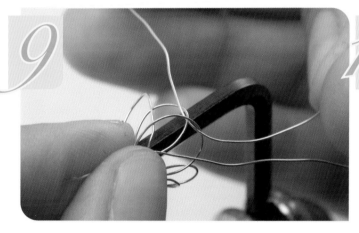

Step 9: Begin threading wire
Thread the working end of the wire through the top two adjacent loops from left to right, and back to the left as you pull it firmly into position so that it starts closing around the wrench. Leave it loose enough to thread the wire underneath again.

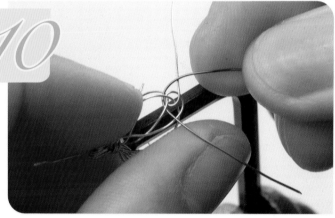

Step 10: Mark start of row
Cut a short length of wire of a different color to use as a marker and thread it through the same two loops that you just connected in step 9. Twist it closed to mark the start of your first row.

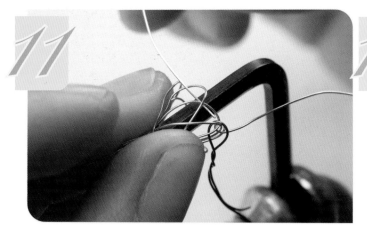

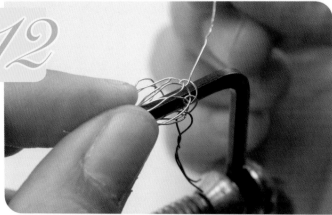

Step 11: Rotate and thread wire

Turn the whole piece toward you a bit and then thread the working end of the wire through two loops: the one counterclockwise of the two you just did, and the one you just did that is adjacent to it.

Step 12: Pull wire

Pull the wire snug and then rotate again.

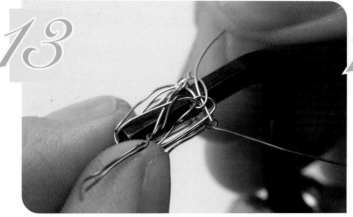

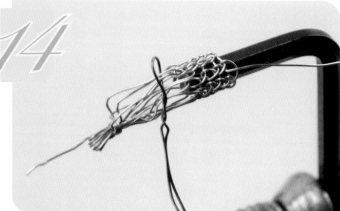

Step 13: Establish rows

When you reach the wire marker, begin the second row by threading the wire through two loops in the row you just completed, just as before.

Step 14: Continue working rows

Continue working rows until you've reached the desired length for the pattern.

Step 15: Remove from hex wrench

Once you are finished with the piece or have arrived at a point in the pattern where you are instructed to switch the wrench size, simply pull the work off. The work will not unravel. Tie a piece of scrap wire through the initial flower loops and twist them together with any other wire ends (the marker, for instance).

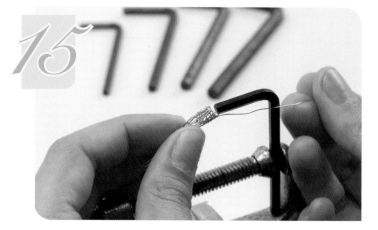

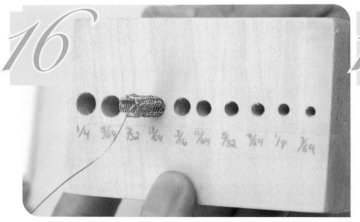

Step 16: Pull through drawplate
Thread the twisted end through the hole in the drawplate that matches the size of the wrench you were using. Firmly but gently, pull the entire work through the hole.

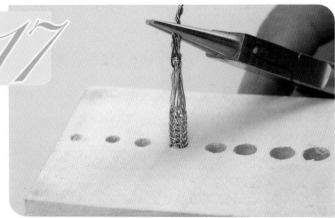

Step 17: Continue to pull
Continue threading the wire through smaller and smaller holes in the drawplate until it has been passed through the instructed hole. The smaller the hole, the harder it is to pull, so you may need to use pliers to assist you. If the wire you're pulling breaks, don't sweat it—that's why you're using the scrap wire you tied to the end. Simply tie another piece in its place to assist you in pulling until the piece passes through.

Tip — *If the rows start getting too compressed and difficult to work with as you knit on the hex wrench, you can use tweezers to separate them.*

STANDARD KNITTING AND CROCHET ABBREVIATIONS

beg	beginning
BO	bind off
cn	cable needle
dec	decrease
foll	following
inc	increase
k	knit
kfb	knit 1 front and back
k2tog	knit 2 together
p	purl
(in) patt	(in pattern)
p2tog	purl 2 together
rem	remaining
rep	repeat
RS	right side
st(s)	stitch(es)
WS	wrong side

TECHNIQUES FOR KNITTED JEWELRY

In addition to basic knitting, you'll also need to learn some simple jewelry techniques repeatedly used throughout the projects in this book. While some are very common and widely used for most jewelry, others are more difficult to adapt to the delicate knitted pieces, so you'll be learning some improvised methods to get around those hurdles.

Wrapping Wire

When I first began knitting jewelry, I noticed that I would need to reinforce the edges (which can look quite unruly and can feel scratchy on your skin) so the work could stand up to regular use. The solution is this simple wire-wrapping process, which results in a finished edge that reinforces your knitted shape and feels smooth to the touch. Although it is easy, wire wrapping your knitted edges does take time, but it's worth the effort to create a stronger, more wearable piece.

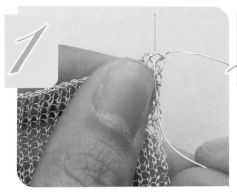
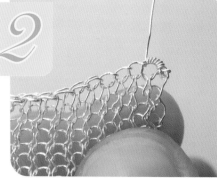
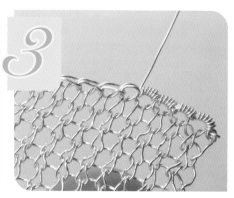

Step 1: Use wire tail to begin first wire wrap
When you bind off your last knitted row, do not trim the tail of the wire flush to the piece. Instead, leave the excess for wire wrapping. Here, for a 1 ⅝" (4.1cm) square, I am leaving about 4" (10cm) of wire. Complete step 7 in Binding Off (page 23) so you have a clean edge that is not flattened. Thread the end of the wire through the first loop at the corner of the bound-off edge. Pull it taut.

Step 2: Cover first loop edge with wire wraps
Repeat until you have 4 or 5 wraps through the first loop, or until the entire exposed edge of that loop is covered.

Step 3: Continue wrapping edge
Continue down the edge in this manner, neatly covering each loop to create a more finished, defined edge to the knitted piece.

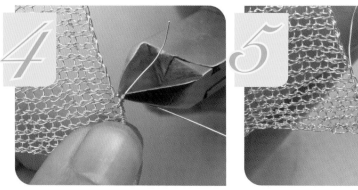
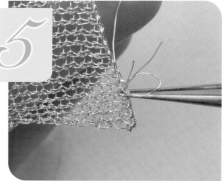

Step 4: Trim wire flush
When you finish the final wrap of any wire-wrapped section or edge, use end cutters to cut the end as close as you can to the loop.

Step 5: Secure wire end
Use tweezers or pliers to tuck the end in, squeezing it flush to the wire. Secure it with a tiny dab of jewelers' cement, epoxy or superglue.

Adding Jump Rings or Clasps at the Beginning

In order to add jump rings and clasps that have been soldered closed, you will need to add them as the piece is being knit and before the piece gets wrapped. Although you can use findings that have *not* been soldered closed and simply add them once the project is finished, this method allows for a more secure connection.

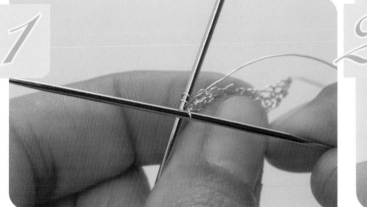

Step 1: Cast on stitches
Cast on the number of stitches needed for the project you're beginning. Slide the cast-on row off the needle.

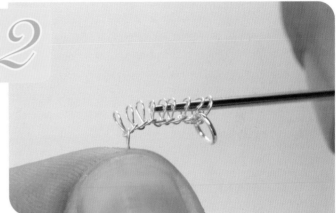

Step 2: Place jump rings
Place jump rings between the stitches where desired. Slide the cast-on row back onto the knitting needle with the jump rings in place.

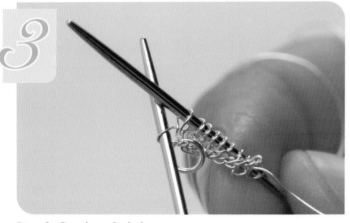

Step 3: Continue knitting
Once placed, continue knitting the next row as usual, trapping the jump rings between the stitches.

Tip Pay careful attention when placing your jump rings. The only way to get them out once you've finished knitting the section is to cut them out.

29

Adding Jump Rings While Binding Off

The result for adding jump rings while binding off is the same as for adding jump rings at the beginning, but the techniques differ slightly. When jump rings are added at the beginning of the piece, they are placed between stitches on the cast-on row; at the end, they are slipped onto individual stitches as the piece is being bound off.

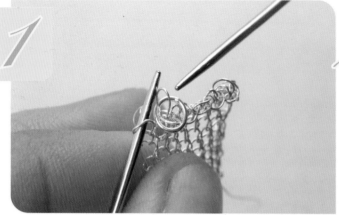

Step 1: Place jump rings
While binding off as usual and once the stitch where the jump ring should go is knit (here it is the second to last stitch), release the right-hand needle and place the jump ring so that the whole stitch is threaded through. Slip right-hand needle back in the stitch.

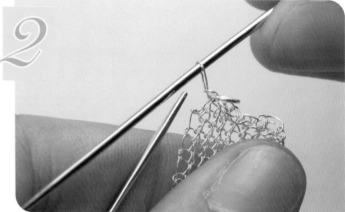

Step 2: Knit and pass stitch over
Knit the next stitch loosely and insert the left-hand needle into the stitch threaded through the jump ring on the right-hand needle, making sure the ring remains underneath the left-hand needle. Pass that stitch over the second knitted stitch (here, the last stitch).

Adding Ear Wires or Clasps at the End of a Piece

Using ear wires that are soldered closed eliminates the threat of melting the delicate knitting when soldering an ear wire closed and guarantees the earring will not fall off the ear wire, should it open accidentally. If you use them, however, you will need to place them onto the earring before the loop gets wire-wrapped. Use this technique when there is just one loop left to bind off. Most earrings in this book are done this way.

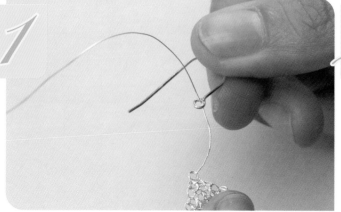

Step 1: Pull out last stitch
After binding off the last stitch, slide it off the needle and pull the loose end toward you (with the knit side facing you), unraveling the stitch halfway, allowing the ear wire to be threaded.

Step 2: Thread through the ear wire
Slide the ear wire onto the wire, making sure the loop faces the front knit side of the earring. Replace the loose end of the wire back through the last stitch and pull the wire until the loop measures about the same as the rest of the stitches below it.

Adding a Separate Wire

This indispensable technique can not only be used as a method to repair a broken wire or as a way to continue knitting if you have reached the end of your length of wire, it can be used creatively to create gaps or different colored stripes in a pattern, as shown here.

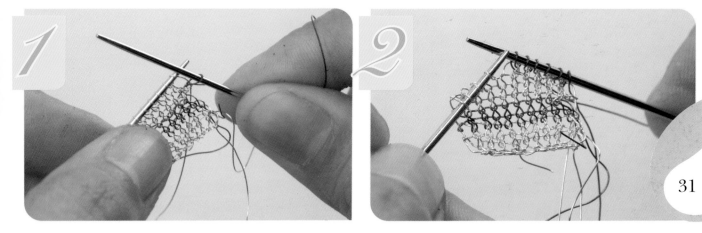

Step 1: Begin knitting with new wire at end of row
When you reach the end of a new row, drop your working wire and add in a new piece of wire (here I'm using this technique to add a stripe of wire in a different color) simply by laying the new wire into position and knitting with it.

Step 2: Leave old wire and continue with new wire
Continue knitting with the new wire for as many rows as desired.

Adding Beads

Adding beads while knitting eliminates the extra wires that would be needed to attach the beads later. It also allows the addition not only of color but of texture. Because this works with almost any beads, it opens the doors for a wide range of possibilities.

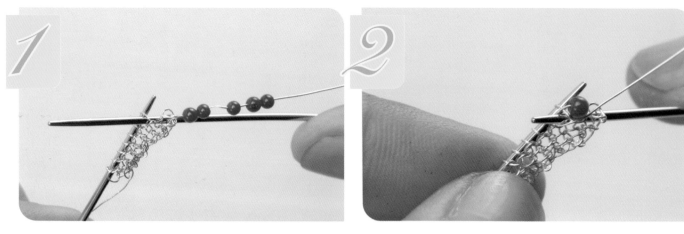

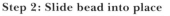

Step 1: String beads onto end of working wire
Cast on the desired number of stitches for your piece. String the beads onto the working wire and tie a loose knot at the end to keep the beads from slipping off.

Step 2: Slide bead into place
When knitting in Stockinette with beads, add the beads only when working on the purl side. The main reason for this is that, on the knit side, there would be no space in the wire lengths (unless you were using incredibly small beads) to house the bead, but the purl side has a longer horizontal bar where the beads can sit.

Once you reach a location where you'd like to add a bead, simply slide the bead up the wire to the needle, then as you begin the purl stitch, wrap the wire around the bead, making sure the bead stays on the near side of the knitted piece.

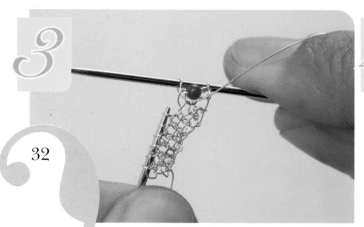

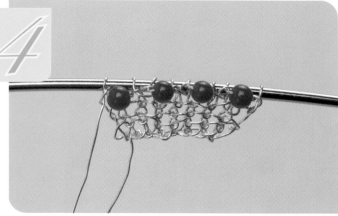

Step 3: Purl, wrapping the bead
Keeping the bead in place, purl the stitch.

Step 4: Add beads as desired
Continue purling beads into place, spacing them as you like.

Wrapping a Loop

Wrapping a loop is an easy way to dangle beads and add jump rings, link together parts in a bracelet, or even to attach a chain or clasp to an already knitted piece. Although it is very simple to do, it is a surprisingly strong and versatile technique even when done with very thin wire.

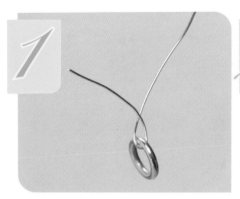

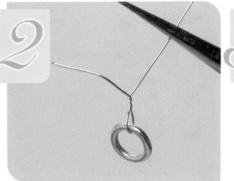

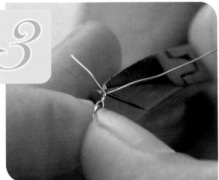

Step 1: Slide first piece onto wire
Bend a short length of wire and slide on whatever object you wish to attach (in this case, a jump ring).

Step 2: Twist wire ends
Twist the ends of the wire together close to the jump ring, using tweezers or pliers, if necessary. The tighter you twist it, the less dangly the item on the wire will be, so adjust your tension according to the desired effect.

Step 3: Trim ends flush
Once the twist is secure, trim the smaller of the two ends flush to the wire.

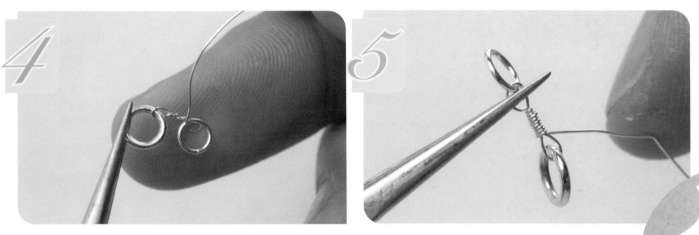

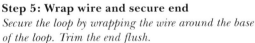

Step 4: Slide second piece onto wire
Slide the object you want to attach onto the remaining wire. Cross the wire over itself to form a loop.

Step 5: Wrap wire and secure end
Secure the loop by wrapping the wire around the base of the loop. Trim the end flush.

Linking Knitted Pieces or Adding Chain

One of the many ways to use a loop, this method allows for joining multiple parts together. It can be applied as a simple means to add a necklace clasp, or to add more dimension to a chain, as in the chandelier-like swoops in the *Lily Necklace* (see page 114).

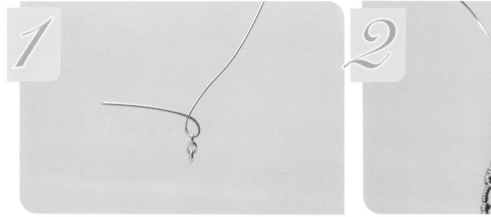

Step 1: Knot short length of chain to wire

Cut a length of chain links. (Here, I'm using very small cable hand-drawn chain, each link about 1mm [.04"] in diameter. If you're using larger chain, you may choose to use fewer links. You need just enough to give each link mobility.) Slide the length of chain onto a 1 ½"–2" (4cm–5cm) length of wire and begin wrapping a loop to secure it (following steps 1–3 on the previous page).

Step 2: Slide wire end through piece to be linked

Slide the remaining wire into the center stitch of the side of one of the knit pieces, crossing the wire over itself to position the chain close to the edge of the stitch.

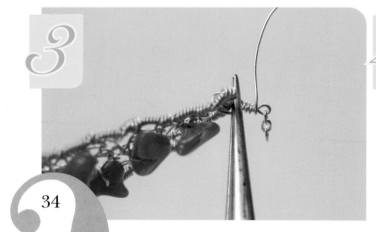

Step 3: Complete loop knot

Complete wrapping the loop to secure it in place.

Step 4: Secure end and repeat

Wrap the wire around and twist to secure loop in place. Repeat the process to attach another link to the other end of the small length of chain in the same way.

Creating Gaps

Creating a gap in the middle of a knitted piece breaks up the space with yet another new design element. By adding a new wire and binding off several of the first stitches in the middle of a row, you can create a gap or hole in the knitting. For illustrative purposes, the example below is from the *Peridot and Iolite Earrings* (see page 70), but the stitch and row counts can easily be adjusted for any knitted pattern that requires a gap.

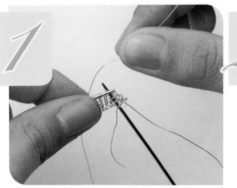 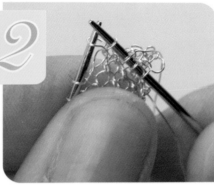 

Step 1: Add second wire
Cast on and knit the number of rows of Stockinette as directed to begin the pattern— in this case, 6. Knit the first few stitches of the row—here, it is 3. Cut a 3' (91cm) piece of wire—this will be Wire 2 in the pattern— and knit the next 2 stitches with Wire 2.

Step 2: Bind off in pattern
With Wire 2, bind off the first of the 2 stitches you just knit by passing it over the other. Knit another stitch, and use it to bind another stitch off. Continue binding off stitches with Wire 2 two more times or as instructed. This will begin the gap. Knit to the end of the row with Wire 2.

Step 3: Purl with each wire
Purl 4 (or however many stitches there are) with Wire 2. Skip over the bound-off rows to the other side and purl 3 (or however many stitches are on this side) with the original wire, or Wire 1.

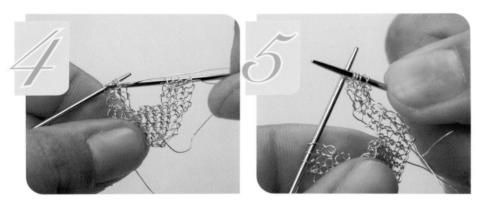

Step 4: Increase and decrease to adjust gap
Increase the amount of stitches at the inner edges to narrow the gap and decrease them to widen it. For the Peridot and Iolite Earrings, *increase stitches to slightly widen the outer edge of the earring, like so: Knit 1 front and back with Wire 1. Knit 2 with Wire 1. Skip to the other side and knit 4 with Wire 2. For the next row: Decrease stitches to slightly widen the gap of the earring, like so: Purl 4 with Wire 2. Purl 2 together and purl to the end of the row with Wire 1. (Photo shows purling 2 together.)*

Step 5: Continue knitting each side
Knit one row using the corresponding wire on each side, as directed.

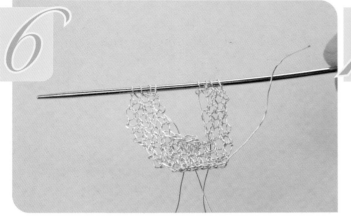

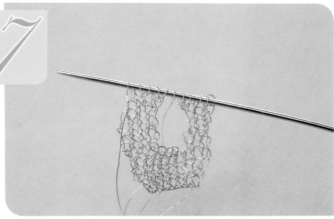

Step 6: Decrease purls, increase knits

Purl 2 together and purl 2 with Wire 2. Purl 3 with Wire 1. Next row: Knit 2 with Wire 1, then increase one stitch by knitting the final stitch front and back. This will begin to decrease the gap. (Photo shows finishing the increase.) Decrease the gap again on the other side by knitting the first stitch front and back with Wire 2. Knit to the end of the row. You now should have 4 stitches on each side.

Step 7: Continue working in pattern

Purl with corresponding wire on each side. Next row: Knit 3 with Wire 1 and knit 1 front and back. With Wire 2, knit 1 front and back and knit to the end of the row. You should now have 5 stitches on each side and you're ready to close the gap on the next row.

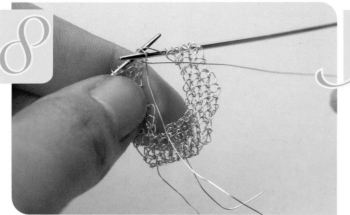

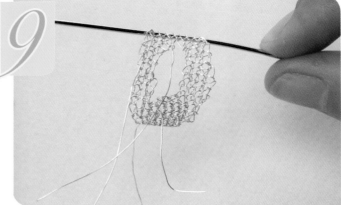

Step 8: Join gap on purl row

Use Wire 2 to purl 2 stitches together and then purl 3, join the gap together, purl another 3, and purl 2 together again. Discard Wire 1 (because you have knit the whole row with Wire 2), but do not cut off—this will be used to wrap the edges of the inside gap later.

Step 9: Finish knitting

Continue working in pattern as normal, with the gap now completely closed.

Tip When designing a piece, if I'm going to decrease a row, I normally try to do it near the beginning of the row because the tension on the wire is more comfortable that way. It also avoids twists that could put so much pressure on the wire that it breaks.

WORKING WITH SHEET METAL

Sheet metal is used in some projects in the book not only for practical or structural uses, but also as integral elements of the designs. By manipulating the flat metal through sawing, forming, drilling, texturing and patinating, you can easily complement or add contrasts to the airy, knit work.

Cutting and Filing a Piece of Sheet Metal

The most important steps when working with raw sheet metal are cutting and filing, because they prepare the surface to be worked. When cutting, accurate measurements are crucial; follow the adage "measure twice and cut once." Once cut, use a file to dull and straighten any less-than-perfect or sharp edges.

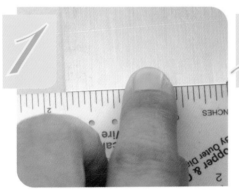

Step 1: Measure and mark sheet
Mark the dimensions of your desired piece using a straightedge and an awl.

Step 2: Saw along marks
Hold your strip of sheet metal firmly over an edge and cut along the outside of your marked lines with a jeweler's saw. (You can also use a clamp, but place a thin piece of wood or cloth between the metal and the clamp so as not to mar the surface.)

Step 3: File until smooth
File all the edges and corners smooth so they won't catch on anything or scratch your skin. Where instructed, round out the corners with the file for an even smoother finish.

Drilling and/or Cutting a Center Opening in Sheet Metal

When a center opening needs to be cut out from a length of sheet metal, it is necessary to drill a hole within the material to be cut out in order to fit the saw blade.

Step 2: Saw around edges of opening
Detach the blade from your jeweler's saw and thread the sheet metal onto it through the hole you just drilled in step 1. Saw around the marks you've drawn, tracking the blade just inside the marks. (You can always file any excess away later.)

Step 1: Mark and drill center
Mark the dimensions for the center opening using a straightedge and an awl. Using a hand drill and a drill bit with a diameter large enough to accommodate your saw blade, drill a hole off-center just inside the marked-off area. Be careful to keep your drill straight up and down and resist the urge to put too much pressure on the drill (it can dull your bit).

Texturing Sheet Metal

By texturing the surface of the metal using several grades of abrasive materials, you can prepare the metal for the application of a patina, erase unintended markings and even change the overall look of the work.

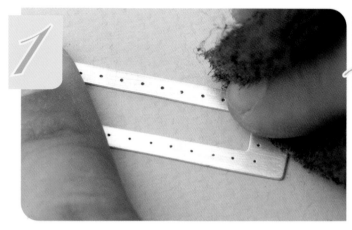

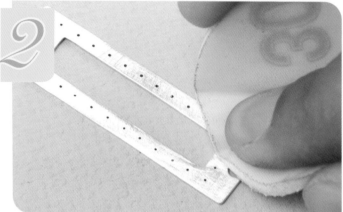

Step 1: Distress surface with scouring pad
Once your piece is cut, filed and/or drilled for the project at hand, use a coarse scouring pad to remove any marks made on the surface of the metal piece.

Step 2: Sand to desired finish
Continue distressing and texturing the surface with a fine-grit sanding pad. Here I'm using a 280-grit piece to create a brushed-steel look.

Forming Sheet Metal or Thick Wire

Sheet metal is used throughout the book in pieces such as rings and bracelets, most of which require forming the flat sheet into curves and circles. Although other tools, such as hammers, are needed to create full circles, the malleability of the metal allows the gentler curves in longer pieces to be made using only your fingers.

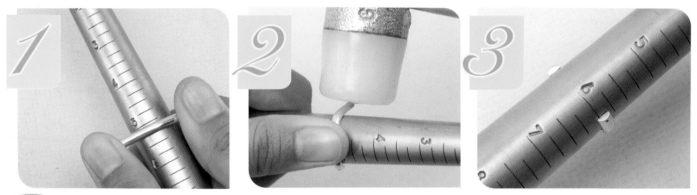

Step 1: Position metal on mandrel
Place a piece of sheet metal or thick wire (a half-round piece of wire for a ring is shown here) over a ring mandrel and align it with a size slightly smaller than the size you want the finished piece to be, centering the wire on the mandrel. Press it around the mandrel with your fingers.

Step 2: Hammer with mallet
Use the mallet to pound the metal flat against the ring mandrel. If you are having a hard time rounding the edges as you work, use the nylon-covered half needle-nose pliers to assist you.

Step 3: Flatten to size
As you flatten the metal, work it down to the size it needs to be to complete the forming of the metal. Because the mandrel is tapered, make sure to remove the piece, flip it over, and work it down again to ensure an even fit.

Polishing Sheet Metal

Although the metal is usually quite shiny when purchased, it is likely to collect a series of marks—from the tools used to create the piece—that will need to be removed. It is helpful to even out the surface first by sanding it with progressively finer sandpaper until it is finally burnished to a deep shine.

Step 1: Distress surface to even finish
Once you've cut, drilled or shaped the metal to the specifications of the project, rub a scouring pad over both the inside and the outside of the metal's surface. If you have shaped the metal, as I have here, this will remove any kinks and marks from hammering and forming.

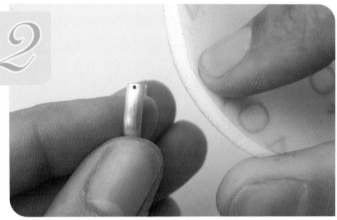

Step 2: Sand surface smooth
Use a fine-grit sandpaper to very lightly continue to smooth the entire surface of the metal. Switch to even finer sandpaper and continue to sand until the whole surface is even.

Step 3: Polish with jewelry cloth
Use a jewelry cloth to begin to work the metal into a shine—apply quite a bit of pressure. You can use a polishing compound to speed up the process.

Step 4: Burnish to desired sheen
Use a burnishing tool with a firm amount of pressure to finish polishing the metal. This is especially useful in polishing more difficult-to-reach places on the inside of the shaped piece of metal, like the ring shown here.

Step 5: Repeat polish
Rub the piece with the polishing cloth once again to even out the sheen made with the burnisher.

Applying a Patina

Although most metals darken or tarnish on their own (silver in particular), applying a darkening patina speeds up the process and has the added advantage of being controllable. Diluted liver of sulfur can be applied with a paintbrush to specific areas, or as in most cases throughout the book, the sheet metal or a length of thin wire can be submerged in the solution. Wax repels the water in the patina, so it can be used to mask areas not meant for it, as in the *Painted Cuff* (page 86); it also protects metal and can be used to coat the patinated work to protect the finish.

Step 1: Submerge metal in liver-of-sulfur solution

If you're working with sheet metal, texture the surface first so it will pick up more color. If you're working with wire, no prior work is required. Simply drop the piece in a diluted solution of liver of sulfur, following the manufacturer's instructions. I like to use warm water to make it develop faster. Leave it in the solution until the desired effect is achieved (5–10 minutes for the look shown here). Remove the piece and rinse it thoroughly with water (liver of sulfur is toxic). Dry it with paper towels.

Step 2: Apply wax

Use your fingers to coat the right side of the piece with wax to ensure the effect of the patina does not rub off on your skin. Work a thick coat into the surface and gently rub away the excess.

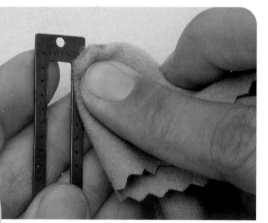

Step 3: Polish wrong side of piece

You'll want to remove the patina from the wrong side of the piece so that it will not rub off on your skin. (If you're working with sheet metal, be sure not to texture the wrong side; it will make this step easier.) Simply rub the surface with a jewelry polishing cloth to reveal the shiny metal beneath the patina.

Before knitting this piece, the length of wire that was recommended for the piece was loosely coiled and then dipped into the diluted liver of sulfur, just like the sheet metal above. After the color developed, the wire was rinsed and thinly coated with wax. It was then treated just as any other wire during the knitting process.

PART TWO
jewelry projects

On the following pages you can see the wide range of applications knitted wire can have when making jewelry.

Because knitting allows you to make a flexible yet stable fabric out of metal, a piece such as the *Lily Necklace* (see page 114) can come to life as you transform a square panel of knitting by bending it into the organic shape of a flower. On the other hand, you can accentuate traditional knitting methods, as I did in the *Patinated Silver Cable Cuff* on page 92, transforming a familiar pattern by exploring its possibilities in metal and allowing the cables to really stand out. Different techniques produce different three-dimensional results, from the sleek and abstract qualities of the *Viking Cuff* (see page 90) to the representational *Flower Ring* (see page 56) and *Butterfly Pendant* (see page 120).

But to me, perhaps the most interesting quality in all these pieces is that, because they are made from hundreds of individual stitches, they are transparent and therefore constantly deceive the eye. Contrasting this visual fragility with the weight and solidity of sheet metal can yield very interesting results, as is the case with pieces such as the *Frame Ring* (see page 50), which suspends two delicate knitted panels in the center of its solid contours.

Although it is satisfying to see a piece of jewelry take form from simple pieces of wire, the ability to explore and push materials and processes to new limits is the greatest reward. Most importantly, the process, which is fascinating on its own, always takes center stage.

RINGS

The challenge for me in designing these rings was to make pieces that did not require soldering and that could be both stylish and durable. Rings have structural limitations in that they have to fit around a finger, but I did not want this to also limit their styles. I wanted to feature the knit work, but I also wanted to explore techniques in sheet metal.

The same basic Stockinette stitch is featured in all the projects, yet its versatility allowed me to explore a great variety of styles. Simple increases and decreases in stitches play a major role in varying the design when paired with a simple, thin band, such as the *Small Double-Textured Ring* (see page 46), and, as in the *Flower Ring* (see page 56), they can create translucent textures when stacked.

Color became another channel for transforming a simple square of sheet metal into an interesting design. For the *Striped Gold Ring* (see page 54), pairing gold and silver added a bit of sparkle to a classic design; contrasting shiny silver with a dark, dull patina added a modern touch to the traditional shape of the *Etched Striped Ring* (see page 48).

In the end, the rings were designed to play with a variety of structures, techniques and styles, from rugged and industrial to dainty and feminine.

SMALL DOUBLE-TEXTURED RING

This tiny ring is one of the best representations of how several techniques can be combined into one project: knitting, increasing and decreasing, wire-wrapping and even incorporating other metals are explored. The pairing of a delicate, knit piece with a bold smooth band creates a contrast of texture, but the work's drama comes from the subtleties created by increasing and decreasing the stitches.

Materials

set of US 0000 (1.25mm) straight knitting needles

30-gauge Argentium or sterling silver wire, about 30" (76cm)

3.2mm × 1.6mm (⅛" × ¹⁄₁₆") Argentium or sterling half-round wire, half hard (2" [5cm] should be plenty for up to a ring size 13)

nylon-covered coiling flat jaw pliers

awl for marking

jeweler's saw

needle files

no. 77 drill bit

hand drill

steel burnisher

ring mandrel

small rubber, nylon or rawhide mallet

scouring pad

sandpaper (very fine) or steel wool

polishing cloth and rouge (if cloth does not already contain compound)

wire cutters

jeweler's tweezers

toothpick or pin (for placement of epoxy)

clear epoxy or jeweler's cement

Pattern

With the 30" (76cm) wire, cast on 1 st.

Row 1: K1.

Row 2: P1.

Row 3: Kfb.

Row 4: P2.

Row 5: K1, kfb.

Row 6: P3.

Row 7: K3.

Row 8: P1, p2tog.

Row 9: K2.

Row 10: P2tog.

Row 11: K1.

Bind off. Wrap the edges of the knitting, making sure to tuck in loose ends.

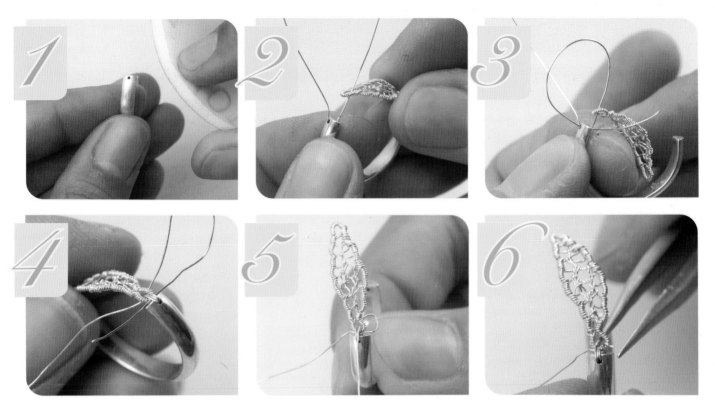

Prepare the Band

With an awl, mark and then use a jeweler's saw to cut the half-round wire to a length that corresponds to your desired ring size, minus the size of the knitted piece (about ¹³⁄₁₆" [2.1cm]). Here I'm using a 1¹¹⁄₃₂" (3.4cm) piece for a size 6 (the length of the inner diameter of a size 6, if rolled out flat, should measure about 2⁵⁄₃₂" (5.5cm). Therefore, 1¹¹⁄₃₂" (3.4cm) half-round wire + ¹³⁄₁₆" (2.1cm) of knitting = 2⁵⁄₃₂" (5.5cm).

File the edges smooth and round. Measure ¹⁄₁₆" (1.6mm) lengthwise from an end of the half-round and mark lightly with an awl. Now, starting at your mark, measure across the width of the half round and mark at half (about ¹⁄₁₆" [1.6mm]). Repeat markings for the opposite side. With a no. 77 bit, drill a hole in each end of the half round at the convergence of the marks. To remove the burrs made while drilling, scratch the edges of the holes with a burnisher. Shape and polish your ring (**Figure 1**) as outlined in *Working with Sheet Metal* or *Forming Sheet Metal or Thick Wire* on pages 37 and 38. (The photos shown on pages 38 and 39 show the *Small Double-Textured Ring* in progress.)

Construct the Ring

Place the knitting on your thumb and with your index and middle fingers, shape it into a slight curve. Cut two 4" (10cm) pieces of 30-gauge Argentium or sterling wire. Thread one wire into one of the holes until the hole is around the wire's midpoint (2" [5cm]). Slide the last loop at one of the tips of the knitted piece (knit side up) down over the one wire and flush against the ring (**Figure 2**). Curl the wire over and back down through the drilled hole in the ring (**Figure 3**).

Alternating the ends of the wire, continue "sewing" the knitted piece to the ring until the wire no longer fits through the hole (about 3 times total). Then, thread one of the wire ends under the loops you just created and pull it taut (**Figure 4**). Thread the other wire end in the opposite direction under the loops (effectively crossing the 2 wire ends), wrap it around the edge of the wrapped knitting and thread it up through the knitting so it looks like another wire wrap (**Figure 5**). Repeat the same process for the other end of the half round.

Cut each wire end close to the ring and use tweezers to press it flush (**Figure 6**). Secure loose ends with a drop of clear epoxy or jeweler's cement.

47

ETCHED STRIPED RING

Materials

set of US 0000 (1.25mm) straight knitting needles

30-gauge Argentium or sterling silver wire (about 60" [152cm])

30-gauge fine or sterling silver wire, darkened and waxed as instructed on page 40 (about 48" [122cm])

ring mandrel

jeweler's saw

small rubber, nylon or rawhide mallet

22-gauge sterling silver sheet (at least ½" × 2" [1cm × 5cm] for up to a ring size 12)

nylon-covered coiling flat jaw pliers

awl for marking

hand drill

no. 77 drill bit

wire cutters

liver of sulfur or other darkening agent, dissolved according to manufacturer's instructions

2 fine-tip soft artist's brushes (size 2/0 or smaller)

Butcher's wax, paint wax or cold wax painting medium

clear epoxy or jeweler's cement

toothpick or pin (for placement of epoxy)

jeweler's tweezers

polishing cloth and rouge (if cloth does not already contain compound)

needle files

fine-grit sanding pad

sandpaper (very fine) or steel wool

steel burnisher

scouring pad

paper towels

I was curious to see how a simple, continuing design would alter in texture and transparency when showcased through both the knit part and the solid silver of a ring. While the ring's shape is bold and sleek, the alternating colors in the knitting as well as the etched stripes make the piece look anything but simple.

Pattern

Cast on 6 sts with patinated silver (PS).

Row 1: K6 with PS; cut, leaving ½" (1cm) tail.

Row 2: Add new Argentium or sterling silver wire (SS) and p6.

Row 3: K6 with SS.

Row 4: P6 with SS; cut, leaving ½" (1cm) tail.

Row 5: Add PS and k6; cut, leaving ½" (1cm) tail.

Row 6: Add SS and p6.

Row 7: K6 with SS; cut, leaving ½" (1cm) tail.

Row 8: Add PS and p6.

Row 9: K6 with PS.

Row 10: P6 with PS; cut, leaving ½" (1cm) tail.

Row 11: Add SS and k6.

Row 12: P6 with SS.

Bind off with SS. Wrap the knitting with the remaining wire.

48

Prepare the Band

Measure and mark the 22-gauge silver sheet to ½" (1cm) wide by the length that would correspond to your ring size minus the length of the knitted piece (about ¾" [1.9cm]). For a ring size 7, the length of the band would be about 1½" (4cm). Cut the sheet to size and file the edges.

Drill 6 holes evenly spaced (about ²⁄₂₅" [2mm] apart and ¹⁄₂₅" [1mm] from the edge) on each end with the hand drill using a no. 77 bit. Polish as outlined on page 39.

Mark and score stripes across the width of the band with an awl according to the following measurements, as shown above (**Figure 1**) for 1½" (4cm) or size 7: ¹⁄₁₆" (1.6mm), ⅛" (3.2mm), ¹⁄₁₆" (1.6mm), ⁵⁄₃₂" (4mm), ³⁄₃₂" (2.4mm), ¹⁄₁₆" (1.6mm), ⁵⁄₃₂" (4mm), ¹⁄₃₂" (.8mm), ³⁄₃₂" (2.4mm), ⁵⁄₃₂" (4mm), ¹⁄₁₆" (1.6mm), ³⁄₃₂" (2.4mm), ⅛" (3.2mm), ¹⁄₁₆" (1.6mm), ³⁄₃₂" (2.4mm), ¹⁄₁₆" (1.6mm).

Leaving the first stripe polished (¹⁄₁₆" [1.6mm]), use an awl to texture every second striped section of the sheet metal (⅛" [3.2mm], ⁵⁄₃₂" [4mm], ¹⁄₁₆" [1.6mm] and so on), working crosshatch scratches into the surface (**Figure 2**). Aim to create the same effect you would by distressing a larger surface with sandpaper.

Use a fine-point paintbrush to brush an even amount of wax onto the untextured stripes of the band (**Figure 3**).

Using the other paintbrush, carefully paint liver of sulfur into the textured stripes (**Figure 4**). Let the solution sit until the desired patina effect is achieved (a dark bluish gray). Then follow instructions for rinsing, brushing with wax and buffing, as outlined in *Applying a Patina* on page 40.

Curve the band around a mandrel as shown in *Forming Sheet Metal or Thick Wire* on page 38.

Construct the Ring

Hold the knitting up to one edge of the formed band, making sure the first stripe of the knitting is not the same color as the first stripe in the band, in order to continue the alternating color scheme.

Cut 2 6" (15cm) pieces of 30-gauge Argentium or sterling wire. Thread one wire into the right corner loop in the knitting and sew through the corresponding drilled hole in the band, leaving a tail just long enough to grab (about 1" [2.5cm]). Continue sewing. Each loop or stitch should have one corresponding drilled hole in the band (6 total). Once sewn, thread the remaining wire ends under the loops you just created, wrap and secure (see *Small Double-Textured Ring* on page 46).

Repeat the process with the other piece of wire at the opposite end.

49

For this piece I tried to design a full cylinder out of sheet metal with which I could frame the knitting—but I didn't want to use a torch. Sewing through drilled holes was the answer, and here it becomes more than a structural aspect; it is also decorative. I further emphasized the contrasts in texture by darkening the wire before knitting and then pairing it with shiny silver.

FRAME RING

Materials

set of US 0000 (1.25mm) straight knitting needles

2 pieces of 30-gauge fine or sterling silver wire, darkened and waxed as instructed on page 40 (about 48" [122cm] each)

ring mandrel

jeweler's saw

small rubber, nylon or rawhide mallet

22-gauge sterling silver sheet (at least ⁷⁄₁₆" [1.1cm] wide and 2⁹⁄₃₂" [5.8cm] long for ring size 7)

nylon-covered coiling flat jaw pliers

awl for marking

hand drill

no. 77 drill bit

wire cutters

liver of sulfur or other darkening agent, dissolved according to manufacturer's instructions

Butcher's wax, paint wax or cold wax painting medium

clear epoxy or jeweler's cement

toothpick or pin (for placement of epoxy)

jeweler's tweezers

polishing cloth and rouge (if cloth does not already contain compound)

needle files

fine-grit sanding pad

sandpaper (very fine) or steel wool

steel burnisher

scouring pad

paper towels

Pattern

Make 2

Cast on 3 sts with one piece of wire.

Rows 1, 3, 5, 7, 9, 11, 13 and 15: K3.

Rows 2, 4, 6, 8, 10, 12 and 14: P3.

Do not bind off.

Do not cut the excess wire. Using the tweezers, twist the last 3 unbound stitches of each piece counterclockwise. They should now face the same way as the rest of the stitches below them.

Prepare the Band

With an awl, measure and mark a rectangle $\frac{7}{16}$" (11.1mm) wide and $2\frac{6}{25}$" (5.7cm) long for a size 7 ($2\frac{7}{50}$" [5.4cm] is the accurate measurement for the inner circumference for a size 7, but adding 3.14 times the thickness of the 22-gauge sheet [about $\frac{1}{40}$" (.64mm)] to the total standard length and an extra $\frac{1}{50}$" [.5mm]—due to the thickness of the band—makes for a better fit). Cut and file edges smooth. Do not round off the corners, as they are meant to join flush once sewn in place.

Once the rectangle has been cut, measure and mark 2 more rectangles within it. Starting $\frac{1}{16}$" (1.6mm) from the edges lengthwise, and $\frac{1}{8}$" (3.2mm) from each edge above and below, the rectangles should each be 1" (2.5cm) × $\frac{3}{16}$" (4.8mm), with a $\frac{1}{8}$" (3.2mm) gap between them in the center. These instructions are for a size 7. If making a different size, follow the *Tip* (page 53) to calculate the length. It's important then to keep the inner rectangle cutouts within the $\frac{1}{32}$" (.8mm) measurement from the short, outer edges, and $\frac{1}{8}$" (3.2mm) from the long outer ones. The inside holes will remain close to the edges of the cutouts, but the distance between these will vary from the $\frac{1}{8}$" (3.2mm) illustrated due to length changes.

Drill a hole with a bit slightly larger than the blade on the saw within the boundaries of each of the 2 rectangles (as outlined on page 37). Thread the saw blade into the new holes and cut out the rectangles. File smooth.

Measure, mark and drill (with a no. 77 bit) 7 holes on the 2 lateral edges of the outer rectangle $\frac{1}{16}$" (1.6mm) apart and $\frac{1}{32}$" (.8mm) from the edge, starting with the middle and leaving $\frac{1}{32}$" (.8mm) between the corners and the first and last holes.

For the inner rectangles, measure, mark and drill 3 holes at each of the smaller inside lateral edges (2 edges), starting by marking the middle first and then the other 2, each also $\frac{1}{16}$" (1.6mm) apart and $\frac{1}{32}$" (.8mm) from the corner.

For the 4 top and bottom edges of the inner rectangles, begin by marking $\frac{1}{32}$" (.8mm) from the corner and then making 16 marks $\frac{1}{16}$" (1.6mm) apart, ending again $\frac{1}{32}$" (.8mm) from the opposing corner. Repeat for the other 3 sides. In all,

there should be a total of 84 holes (see Illustration 1). Sand the surfaces smooth and then polish (as outlined on page 39).

Holding the sheet-metal band vertically, place 1 of the knit panels (making sure it's knit side up, with the unbound stitches at the top) inside the upper rectangle cutout. Pull the loose wire (which should be on the right side) toward you and then insert through the stitch and pass it under, guiding it to the right and up through the first drilled hole. Continue to sew clockwise through the stitches and their corresponding holes. Stop at the top left corner (the unbound side). Flip the band so the sewn panel is at the bottom with the cast-on row facing the top, and repeat for the other rectangle. You should now have all sides sewn except for the top of one rectangle and the bottom of the other.

Form the band around the ring mandrel with the knit side on the outside as outlined on page 38.

Construct the Ring

With the seam of the ring running vertically, you will now sew not only the final edges of the knitting to the sheet metal, but the 2 edges of the sheet metal together. Starting at the top left corner of the knitting, run the remaining end wire from the knitting under and then through the top left hole on the sheet (A). (See illustration 2.)

Run the wire over the seam and into the opposing hole (H) on the top right side.

Now run the wire diagonally left under the seam toward and up through the second hole down on the left (B). Sew over to the right and down through its opposing hole (I).

Pass the wire under the seam again toward the left and up through the third hole (C).

This time, pass it left over the edge of the inner left rectangle and into the first unbound stitch on the left side.

Moving right, pass the wire under holes and seam and up through the mirroring unbound stitch on the right side.

Sew over the edge of the inner right rectangle and into the third hole on the right side (J).

Moving left again, pass the wire under the seam diagonally and come up into the middle left unbound stitch.

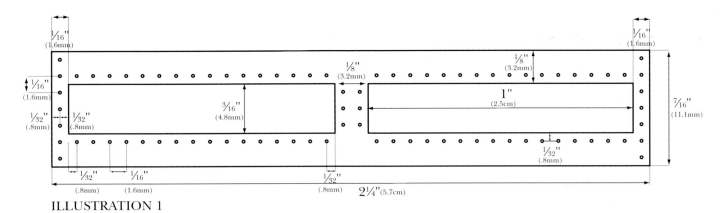

ILLUSTRATION 1

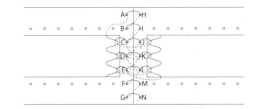

ILLUSTRATION 2

Sew up over the edge and into the fourth hole on the left (D).

Pass the wire under the seam directly across and up through the opposite stitch, the middle right.

Sew wire into the adjoining hole, fourth on the right (K).

Moving left, pass wire under the seam diagonally and up through the third unbound stitch on the left side.

Sew the wire into the fifth hole on the left (E).

Pass it right under the seam and up through the third unbound stitch on the right side.

Sew the wire down through the fifth hole on the right side (L) and pass it left diagonally toward the sixth hole on the left side (F).

Pass it up through (F) and sew it right over the seam and into the opposing hole, the sixth on the right side (M).

Moving left, pass the wire under the seam and up through the last hole on the left (G).

Sew the wire toward the right, passing over the seam and into the last hole on the right (N).

Loop the wire around the underside stitches, cut closely and tuck in with tweezers.

Now, using the remaining wire from the unbound knit panel on the *right* side of the seam, move left under the seam, threading the wire up through (E).

From (E), pass the wire to the right over into (L).

From (L), pass it toward the left, again under the seam, up through (D).

From (D), pass it over the seam into (K).

From (K), pass it under the seam left up through (C).

From (C), pass it over the seam into (J).

Finally, pass the wire under through the stitches and cut, tucking in ends with tweezers. Pass the remaining wire on the right side around any of the wires on the inside of the ring. Cut and tuck in. With a toothpick, place beads of epoxy or cement on any loose ends.

53

STRIPED GOLD RING

Materials

set of US 0000 (1.25mm) straight knitting needles

28-gauge Argentium, sterling silver or silver craft wire (about 2½' [76cm])

28-gauge gold craft wire (about 3½' [107cm])

ring mandrel

jeweler's saw

small rubber, nylon or rawhide mallet

22-gauge sterling silver sheet (at least 3/16" [4.8mm] wide and 2¼" [5.7cm] long for up to a ring size 14)

nylon-covered coiling flat jaw pliers

awl for marking

hand drill

no. 75 drill bit

wire cutters

clear epoxy or jeweler's cement

toothpick or pin (for placement of epoxy)

jeweler's tweezers

polishing cloth and rouge (if cloth does not already contain compound)

needle files

sandpaper (very fine) or steel wool

steel burnisher

scouring pad

Not quite feminine, but definitely not rugged, this refined, two-toned ring is for those who like to wear both gold and silver. Its straightforward shape allows the focus to remain on the color and texture changes. It represents a more traditional, classic style.

Pattern

Cast on 3 sts with silver wire (S).

Row 1: K3 with S.

Row 2: P3 with S; cut, leaving ½" (1cm) tail.

Row 3: Add gold wire (G) and k3.

Row 4: P3 with G.

Row 5: K3 with G.

Row 6: P3 with G; cut, leaving ½" (1cm) tail.

Row 7: Add S and K3.

Row 8: P3 with S.

Row 9: K3 with S.

Do not bind off.

With the remaining gold wire, wrap the edges of the knitting, making sure to tuck in loose ends. Cut ends, tuck in flush and place a bead of epoxy to seal.

Prepare the Band

Measure and mark the silver sheet, making sure to keep the width to ³⁄₁₆" (4.8mm) and then measuring the length that would correspond to your ring size, subtracting the length of the knitted piece (about ¹¹⁄₁₆" [1.7cm]). For a ring size 6.5, the length of the band would be about 1½" (4cm). Cut the sheet to size and file the edges smooth.

At one end of the sheet, divide the width (³⁄₁₆" [4.8mm]) and mark with an awl at 3 equally spaced points, making sure the marks are at least ¹⁄₁₆" (1.6mm) in from the edge. Drill holes into each of these marks with a no. 75 bit and then repeat the process at the other end of the band.

Shape and polish the band as outlined on pages 38 and 39.

Construct the Ring

Cut any remaining gold wire not used in the knitting or wrapping into two equal pieces. Pass the first piece of wire through the middle hole in the band until the band is around the wire's midpoint. Place the knitting, knit side up, against the edge of the sheet metal and pass the wire over the edge and into the middle loop, or stitch, in the knitting directly in front of it. Now, on the inside of the ring, pass it again to the sheet metal side and up through the middle hole. Once on the top, thread it down through the middle stitch (there should now be 2 wires going into the middle stitch) but this time moving left under the

seam and up through the hole left of center in the band. Once up through the hole left of center, pass it over the edge down through the left stitch. Sew it under and then up through the left hole and down through the left stitch one more time so the left hole will now have 2 wires going through it. Leave the wire for now.

Grab the other end in the middle and, moving it to the right under the seam, pass it up through the hole on the right. Once through, sew it into the stitch directly in front of it (right of center). Pass it again under the seam and up one more time through the hole on the right and down through the right stitch. There should now be 2 wires going through the hole.

Thread the left wire under the loops you just created, moving to the right, and pull. Thread the right wire end in the opposite direction under the same loops and wrap it around the side and through the knitting. Repeat wrapping with the other end. The wires should now look like they are part of the border wrapping. Cut and tuck in the ends with tweezers.

Shape the knitting with your fingers into a slight curve, as if to continue the circle, until the other end touches the other edge of the sheet metal band. Sew the knitting into the band as discussed above and seal the loose ends with small beads of epoxy.

FLOWER RING

Materials

set of US 0000 (1.25mm) straight knitting needles

30-gauge Argentium or sterling silver wire (about 13' [396cm])

3 faceted garnet round beads (3mm [³⁄₂₅"]) or similar beads

ring mandrel

jeweler's saw

small rubber, nylon or rawhide mallet

3.1mm × 1.6mm (⅛" × ¹⁄₁₆") Argentium or sterling half-round wire, half hard (3" [7.6cm] should be plenty for up to a ring size 14)

nylon-covered coiling flat jaw pliers

awl for marking

hand drill

no. 77 drill bit

wire cutters

clear epoxy or jeweler's cement

toothpick or pin (for placement of epoxy)

jeweler's tweezers

polishing cloth and rouge (if cloth does not already contain compound)

needle files

sandpaper (very fine) or steel wool

steel burnisher

scouring pad

Inspired by the cocktail rings worn during the '50s and '60s, I designed this extravagant ring by building layers of dainty, lacy petals crowned around a cluster of garnets. The flower itself is made up of six petals, created by following two different patterns. Although the band does go all the way around the finger, there is no need to solder it because the shank is kept closed by sewing the two ends together as the petals are attached (see photo on page 57).

56

Tip If you cut this band to the exact length of the inside circumference needed, it will be too short because the ring gets smaller when you force the ends together. You will have to compensate for the thickness of the half round when measuring. Multiplying the thickness of the band by 3.14 and then adding the resulting figure to the standard length helps to resolve the issue.

Pattern

Cut the 30-gauge wire into six pieces measuring 2' (61cm) each, leaving 1' (30cm) extra.

Make 3 Lower Petals:

Cast on 2 sts.

Row 1: K2.

Row 2: P2.

Row 3: K1, kfb = 3.

Row 4: P3.

Row 5: K3.

Row 6: P2tog, p1 = 2.

Row 7: K2tog = 1.

Bind off.

Make 3 Upper Petals:

Cast on 2 sts.

Row 1: K1, kfb = 3.

Row 2: P3.

Row 3: K3.

Row 4: P2tog, p1 = 2.

Row 5: K2tog = 1.

Bind off.

Wrap all pieces with the extra wire. Cut the wires flush, tuck them in with tweezers and secure them with a bead of epoxy.

Prepare the Band

Measure and mark the half-round wire with an awl at the appropriate length for your desired ring size. For a size 5, the wire would measure 54.324mm (2⁷⁄₅₀") (the thickness of the wire is ¹⁄₁₆" [1.6mm] × 3.14 + 2" [49.3mm] for a size 5 = 2⁷⁄₅₀" [54.324mm]) (see *Tip* on opposite page).

Cut and file edges smooth, being careful not to round them, as they are meant to fit flush. With an awl, make a mark ¹⁄₁₆" (1.6mm) in from the edge of one of the ends. At that point, going across the width of the wire, measure and divide with 3 equally spaced marks about ¹⁄₃₂" (.8mm) apart. Repeat markings at the other end. With a no. 77 bit, drill holes into all 3 marks at both ends.

Form the wire to shape and polish as outlined on pages 37 and 38.

Construct the Ring

With the knit sides up, arrange the Lower Petals evenly around one point, their cast-on rows all pointing toward the center (it should resemble a 3-pointed star). Cut 3" (8cm) of wire and pass it halfway though 1 of the cast-on stitches. Sew the loose ends through the other cast-on rows. Once they are all sewn together, pull the ends tight. Repeat with the Upper Petals. You should have 2 pieces each with 3 petals.

Again with the knit sides up, layer the Upper Petals on top of the Bottom Petals, threading the 2 wire ends of the Upper Petals into the center of the Bottom Petals. Position the Upper Petals between the Bottom Petals. Pull down on the Upper Petal wires to tighten the structure and then wrap the loose ends around the nearest edge of a Bottom Petal, mimicking the wrapping. Now thread the wires belonging to the Bottom Petals up through the middle of the Upper Petals, and again wrap the ends tight around the edges of the Upper Petals. Cut the wires, tuck them into the wrapping with tweezers and seal with a bead of epoxy or jeweler's cement. You should now have 1 flower.

Holding the band so the seam runs vertically (with 3 holes on each side), thread one end of a 6" (15cm) piece of wire through the middle hole on the left side up to the outside. Thread the other end, also from the inside, up through the middle hole on the right side. You should now have 2 wire ends sticking out through the outer side of the band. Align the ends and pull together so both are of equal length.

Thread these 2 ends up through the middle of the flower, making sure the knit side remains at the top. Once at the top and in the middle, thread one bead onto each of the wires and sew them back down through the flower. Guide the right wire down through the top hole on the left side and tightly sew it up through the top hole on the right. Do the opposite with the other wire, guiding it under the flower down through the bottom right hole and sewing it up through the bottom left hole.

Sew one wire up through the middle of the flower to the top. Add the third bead and thread the wire back down through the flower. Sew the wire around the loops, cut, tuck in with tweezers and place a bead of epoxy. With the other wire, wrap the base of the flower tightly and sew into an edge, cut and tuck with tweezers. Seal with epoxy.

EARRINGS

Unlike rings, necklaces and bracelets, earrings are suspended from the body, allowing light to shine through. This makes them a showcase for the delicate properties that make knitted wire jewelry so unique. Plain, sleek contours make bright gemstones pop; cave-like crevices frame dangling jewels while still allowing them to sparkle.

The biggest design benefit to knit earrings, however, is weight and its relationship with size. Because the earrings in this book are knit from such fine wire, they are practically weightless. This allows for larger, bolder designs, without uncomfortable heaviness. The twin gems of the *Opal Rectangle Earrings* (page 62) would make the earrings rather heavy were it not for the light knitwork that supports them.

These sweet and simple hoop earrings, when worn, combine the slightest glitter with an understated, polished shape. When flat, the knit piece is almost rectangular, with only a slight taper at one end. They are incredibly easy to make and comfortable to wear, as they practically float from your ear.

SMALL HOOPS

Materials

Set of US 0000 (1.25mm) straight knitting needles

30-gauge Argentium or sterling silver soft round wire (about 8' [244cm]) cut into 2 4' (122cm) pieces

2 ear nuts 18.4mm × 10mm (.72" × .4") that fit post diameter .66mm–.9mm (.026"–.036")

21-gauge Argentium or sterling silver wire, half hard (about 1½" [4cm]) or 2 posts with a diameter of .66mm–.91mm (.026"–.036") and 3.8cm (1½") long

needle- or round-nose pliers

wire cutters

clear epoxy or jeweler's cement

toothpick or pin (for placement of epoxy)

jeweler's tweezers

polishing cloth and rouge (if cloth does not already contain compound)

needle files

steel burnisher

scouring pad

Pattern

Make 2

Cast on 3 sts.

Rows 1, 3, 5, 7, 9, 11, 13, 15, 17, 19 and 21: K3.

Rows 2, 4, 6, 8, 10, 12, 14, 16, 18 and 20: P3.

Row 22: P2tog, p1.

Row 23: K2tog.

Bind off (add ear wires while binding off, as outlined on page 31, if using posts that are already soldered closed).

Do not cut off excess wire. Instead use the wires to wrap edges. Cut the wires close to the edge and use tweezers to tuck them in flush to the other wires. Secure with a bead of epoxy.

Construct the Earrings

If you're making your own posts, measure 2 sections ¾" (1.9cm) long on the 21-gauge wire and mark with an awl. Cut with a jeweler's saw for a straight line. File one end flat on each of the wires eliminating any angles or bevels made while cutting (this makes measuring easier). Measure the wires against each other to make sure they are equal in length, using the newly flat edges as a reference. File the opposite ends round and smooth.

With the tip of the needle-nose pliers, make a loop at the ends with the flattened edges, pushing the flat edges against the wires. The loops should look more or less like the letter *b*. Polish the pieces as outlined on page 39.

If you're making your own posts or are using premade posts that are not soldered shut, twist the polished loop open (with the loop facing down) and insert the bound-off stitch of one of the knit pieces, making sure the knit side faces away from the post. Close the loop with pliers and repeat for the other post.

To attach the ear nuts, open one of the "wings" on an ear nut with the pliers and thread it through the purl side of the middle stitch of the cast-on row at the opposite end. Close the "wing" up over the edge on the knit side. Repeat the process with the other knitted piece and ear nut and close the hoops.

Modern and breezy, these dangly earrings are an example of how knitted jewelry allows for the addition of heavier gemstones while maintaining the earrings' light weight. The project also shows how the easy Stockinette stitch can be interesting even in the simplest of forms. As with the *Small Double-Textured Ring* (see page 46), decreasing subtly shapes the work.

OPAL RECTANGLE EARRINGS

Materials

set of US 0000 (1.25mm) straight knitting needles

30-gauge Argentium or sterling silver soft round wire (about 8½' [259cm]) cut into 2 4' (122cm) pieces for knitting and wrapping plus 6" (15cm) for adding the beads

2 French ear wires .028" (.7mm) approximately 1" × ½" (2.5cm × 1cm)

needle- or round-nose pliers

wire cutters

clear epoxy or jeweler's cement

toothpick or pin (for placement of epoxy)

jeweler's tweezers

2 Peruvian Opal (or other) pear-cut briolette beads approximately 5mm × 7mm (⅕" × 9/32"), top-drilled

Pattern

Make 2

Cast on 3 sts.

Rows 1, 3, 5, 7, 9, 11, 13, 15, 17, 19, 21, 23 and 25: K3.

Rows 2, 4, 6, 8, 10, 12, 14, 16, 18, 20, 22 and 24: P3.

Row 26: P2tog, p1.

Row 27: K2tog.

Add ear wires while binding off (if soldered closed), as outlined on page 31.

Do not cut the extra wire. Instead use it to wrap the edges. If using soldered ear wires, you will need to wrap through the ear wire in order to continue wrapping around it.

Construct the Earrings

If the ear wires used were not soldered closed, twist them open and insert the knitting, making sure the cast-on edge remains at the bottom and that the knit side faces the front. Press closed with the pliers.

Cut a 3" (7.6cm) piece of wire and thread through the drilled hole at the top of the bead, leaving a ½" (1cm) tail. To wrap a loop, cross the 2 ends and twist (see page 33). Cut the shorter end close to the twist.

Thread the loose end of the wire through the middle opening in the cast-on edge; leaving a bit of space for the bead to dangle, close the wire down toward the bead. Wrap the loose wire around the twist made to hold the bead. Cut the wire. With tweezers, press down flush. Place a bead of epoxy to seal.

Repeat the process for the matching earring.

63

Although a lot of my work references nature in a more abstract manner, it is also possible to use the same techniques for some quite detailed, more realistic pieces—in this case, a leaf skeleton. The knit pattern is quite simple, and you'll find the leaves truly take form once the veins have been made.

LEAF EARRINGS

Materials

set of US 0000 (1.25mm) straight knitting needles

30-gauge Argentium or sterling silver wire (about 6' [183cm]) cut into 2 3' (91cm) pieces

30-gauge gold wire—1 each for the wrapping and sewing (about 10' [305cm]) cut into 2 5' (152cm) pieces

2 French ear wires 0.028" (.7mm) approximately 1" × ½" (2.5cm × 1cm)

needle- or round-nose pliers

wire cutters

clear epoxy or jeweler's cement

toothpick or pin (for placement of epoxy)

jeweler's tweezers

Pattern

Make 2

Cast on 1 st.

Row 1: K1.

Row 2: P1.

Row 3: Kfb = 2.

Row 4: P2.

Row 5: Kfb twice = 4.

Row 6: P4.

Row 7: Kfb, k2, kfb = 6.

Row 8: P6.

Row 9: Kfb, k4, kfb = 8.

Row 10: P8.

Row 11: Kfb, k6, kfb = 10.

Row 12: P10.

Row 13: K10.

Row 14: P10.

Row 15: K2tog, k6, k2tog = 8.

Row 16: P2tog, p4, p2tog = 6.

Row 17: K2tog, k2, k2tog = 4.

Row 18: P2tog, p2tog = 2.

Row 19: K2tog.

Row 20: P1.

Add ear wires while binding off (if soldered closed), as outlined on page 31.

Complete the Earrings

Wrap each of the earrings with gold wire. Start at the point where the silver wire was bound off—the last loop containing the ear wire. Add the new gold wire by straddling the inside and outside edges of the loop and the trailing silver wire and then wrapping over, making sure to include the new end of gold wire. Continue to wrap until all edges are covered, including the ear-wire loop. (Note: If using ear wires that have been soldered closed, it will be necessary to wrap through the ear wire in order to continue wrapping around it.) Clip the gold wire close to the piece (**Figure 1**), tuck in with tweezers (**Figure 2**) and apply a drop of epoxy.

Main Vein

Once the first piece is wrapped, cut a length of gold wire to about 18" (46cm). Temporarily wrap one end of the wire around the top loop containing the ear wire. Run the loose end along the middle of the leaf to the other end lengthwise. Sew the wire around the wrapped edge of this bottom loop (**Figure 3**) and then pass it under and over the new gold "vein," starting the wrapping. As you wrap, occasionally pick up one of the silver wire loops underneath so the vein is stitched to the leaf (**Figure 4**). Continue until the last 3 stitches that make up the "stem" are reached. Unwrap the end from the edge of the loop at the top and sew around the bottom of the third stitch from the top. Cut and tuck. With the loose end, wrap to the end, cut, tuck and place a small bead of epoxy to seal.

Side Veins

Cut a piece of wire about 6" (15cm) long. Beginning on the knit side of the leaf, sew the wire under the middle vein about 3 stitches down from the bottom of the "stem" and pull it back through to the front on the other side so that half of this new wire is now on either side of the middle vein (**Figure 5**). Secure one end by loosely wrapping it over the edge. Run the loose end diagonally across the knitting to the edge, making sure it lies relatively parallel to the bottom of the leaf on that same side. Sew wire around the edge (**Figure 6**), passing under and around the new diagonal vein for the first wrap. Continue in this manner, picking up some of the "leaf" stitches along the way (**Figure 7**), until you reach the middle vein. Cut, tuck and glue. Repeat with the opposite loose end (**Figure 8**), ending with an elongated *V*.

Repeat this process to create two more veins, this time beginning 5 stitches from the center of the *V* along the main vein, making sure the new veins parallel the others.

Repeat the entire veining process for the second earring.

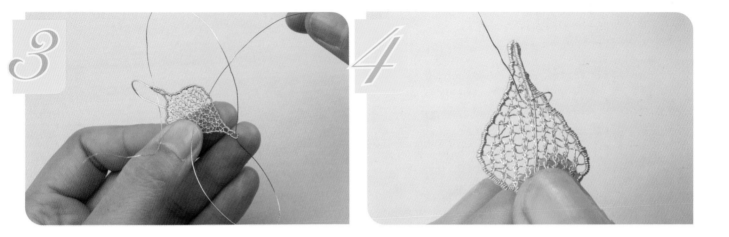

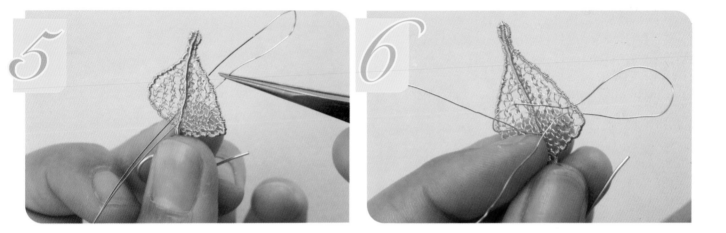

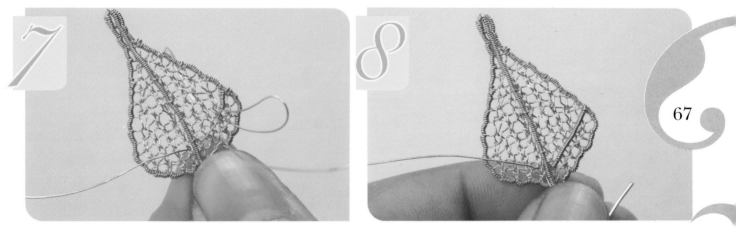

67

Gravity played a major role in the design of these earrings. The addition of chain added a flowing movement and also reinforced the teardrop shape. To give each earring even more weight, I arranged the beads in a gradient before threading them. The result is that, when knit, the darker, heavier colors settle at the bottom in larger numbers, giving way to the lighter, sparser ones at the top.

GRADIENT DROP EARRINGS

Materials

- set of US 0000 (1.25mm) straight knitting needles

- 30-gauge Argentium or sterling silver soft round wire (about 14' [427cm]) divided into 2 6' (183cm) lengths and 2 12" (30.5cm) pieces

- 42 multicolor tourmaline abacus beads, arranged into 2 color gradients of 21 stones each (about 3mm [³⁄₂₅"] in diameter each)

- 2 French ear wires 0.028" (.7mm) approximately 1" × ½" (2.5cm × 1cm)

- 2 lengths of Argentium or sterling silver 1mm (.04") round cable chain about 1⅜" (3.5cm) long (or about 33 links each)

- needle- or round-nose pliers

- wire cutters

- clear epoxy or jeweler's cement

- toothpick or pin (for placement of epoxy)

- jeweler's tweezers

Pattern

String 21 beads onto one of the 6' (183cm) pieces of wire, starting with the darkest bead, which you will knit in first, and finishing with the lightest, which will go last. Make a loose knot at the end of the wire with the light beads so they don't slip out while knitting.

See *Adding Beads* as outlined on page 32.

There is a point in the pattern where another wire is added and partially bound off to create a gap; thus there will be two wires being knit simultaneously. Refer to *Creating Gaps* (page 35) for more detailed instructions.

Make 2

Cast on 7 sts with the beaded wire.

Row 1: K7.

Row 2: [P1, p1 adding bead] 3 times; p1 = 7.

Row 3: Kfb, k5, kfb = 9.

Rows 4, 6, 8 and 10: [P1, p1 adding bead] 4 times; p1 = 9.

Rows 5, 7 and 9: K9.

Row 11: K3, add new wire (W2), BO 3 with W2, k3 = 6.

Row 12: P1, p1 adding bead, p1 with W2; p1, p1 adding bead, p1 with original wire (W1) = 6.

Row 13: K2tog, k1 with W1; k1, k2tog with W2 = 4.

Row 14: P2tog with W2; p2tog with W1 = 2.

Bind off with W1.

Bind off with W2.

Because each earring will have 2 points at which the wire was bound off, pick the longest wire and use it to wrap the edges of the knitting. Cut the wires, tuck in and place a drop of epoxy to seal.

Complete the Earrings

Once both pieces have been wrapped, cut a 1" (2.5cm) length from any remaining wire, thread it through a link at the end of a chain and bend, crossing the ends of the wire. Twist the wires a couple times and cut the shorter end close to the twist (see page 33 for more on wrapping a loop). Take the chain with the loop and insert the loose wire through the top left stitch in the knit piece. Leaving room for movement, close the loop around the edge of the stitch and wrap the wire around the twisted portion. Cut the wire close, tuck in with tweezers and place a drop of epoxy. Repeat for the top right stitch and the other end of the chain.

Thread a 1" (2.5cm) piece of wire through the middle link of the chain. Tie a loop, this time incorporating an ear wire if using those that have been soldered closed. Otherwise close the loop first and attach the ear wire afterward.

Repeat for the other earring.

Inspired by sparkling geodes, the natural and organic shape of these earrings make them at once casual and elegant. The central gap is established by adding a separate wire in the middle of the knitting and then binding off a few stitches. Its shape is then widened and narrowed by increasing and decreasing stitches along its edges. Two separate patterns, one for each earring, make the earrings mirrors for each other, giving the viewer a sense of symmetry.

PERIDOT AND IOLITE EARRINGS

Materials

set of US 0000 (1.25mm) straight knitting needles

30-gauge Argentium or sterling silver soft round wire (about 14' [427cm]) divided into 2 6' (183cm) lengths for the knitting and wrapping and 1 24" (61cm) piece for adding beads

2 peridot pear-cut briolettes (or other suitable stones) about 3mm × 6mm (³⁄₂₅" × ⁶⁄₂₅"), top-drilled

2 iolite smooth teardrops (or other suitable stones) about 4.5mm × 9mm (⁹⁄₅₀" × ⁹⁄₂₅"), top-drilled

2 French ear wires 0.028" (.7mm) wire approximately 1" × ½" (2.5cm × 1cm)

needle- or round-nose pliers

wire cutters

clear epoxy or jeweler's cement

toothpick or pin (for placement of epoxy)

jeweler's tweezers

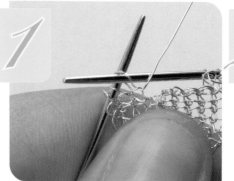
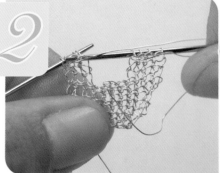
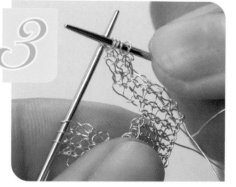

Pattern

Because these shapes are more organic, it is necessary to follow two patterns in order for the earrings to appear symmetrical when worn.

In this pattern, a second wire is added halfway into the row, and the next few stitches are bound off with the new wire to create space. Both wires are knitted simultaneously for a period of time to create a gap. To close the gap, one of the wires is dropped, and the other is used to continue the pattern. Please refer to *Creating Gaps* as outlined on page 35 for more detailed information.

Knitting Pattern A

Cast on 8 sts.

Row 1: K8.

Row 2: P8.

Row 3: Kfb, k6, kfb = 10.

Row 4: P10.

Row 5: K9, kfb = 11.

Row 6: P11.

Row 7: K3, add new wire (W2), BO4, k4 = 7.

Row 8: P4 with W2; p3 with original wire (W1) **(Figure 1)**.

Row 9: Kfb, k2 with W1; k4 with W2 = 8.

Row 10: P4 with W2; p2tog **(Figure 2)**, p2 with W1 = 7.

Row 11: K3 with W1; k4 with W2.

Row 12: P2tog, p2 with W2; p3 with W1 = 6.

Row 13: K2, kfb **(Figure 3)** with W1; kfb, k2 with W2 = 8 **(Figure 4).**

Row 14: P4 with W2; p4 with W1.

Row 15: K3, kfb with W1; kfb, k3 with W2 = 10 **(Figure 5)**.

Row 16: P2tog, p6 **(Figure 6)**, p2tog with W2, dropping W1 = 8 **(Figure 7)**.

Row 17: K8.

Row 18: P6, p2tog = 7.

Row 19: K5, k2tog = 6.

Row 20: P4, p2tog = 5.

Row 21: K3, k2tog = 4.

Row 22: P2, p2tog = 3.

Row 23: K1, k2tog = 2.

Row 24: P2tog = 1.

Add ear wire while binding off (if soldered closed), as outlined on page 31.

Knitting Pattern B

Cast on 8 sts.

Row 1: K8.

Row 2: P8.

Row 3: Kfb, k6, kfb = 10.

Row 4: P10.

Row 5: Kfb, k9 = 11.

Row 6: P11.

Row 7: K4, add new wire (W2), BO4, k3 = 7.

Row 8: P3 with W2; p4 with original wire (W1).

Row 9: K4 with W1; k2, kfb with W2 = 8.

Row 10: P2, p2tog with W2; p4 with W1 = 7.

Row 11: K4 with W1; k3 with W2.

Row 12: P3 with W2; p2, p2tog with W1 = 6.

Row 13: K2, kfb with W1; kfb, k2 with W2 = 8.

Row 14: P4 with W2; p4 with W1.

Row 15: K2tog, k1, kfb with W1; kfb, k3 with W2 = 9.

Row 16: P2tog, p7 with W2, dropping W1 = 8.

Row 17: K8.

Row 18: P2tog, p6 = 7.

Row 19: K2tog, k5 = 6.

Row 20: P2tog, p4 = 5.

Row 21: K2tog, k3 = 4.

Row 22: P2tog, p2 = 3.

Row 23: K2tog, k1 = 2.

Row 24: P2tog = 1.

Add ear wire while binding off (if soldered closed), as outlined on page 31.

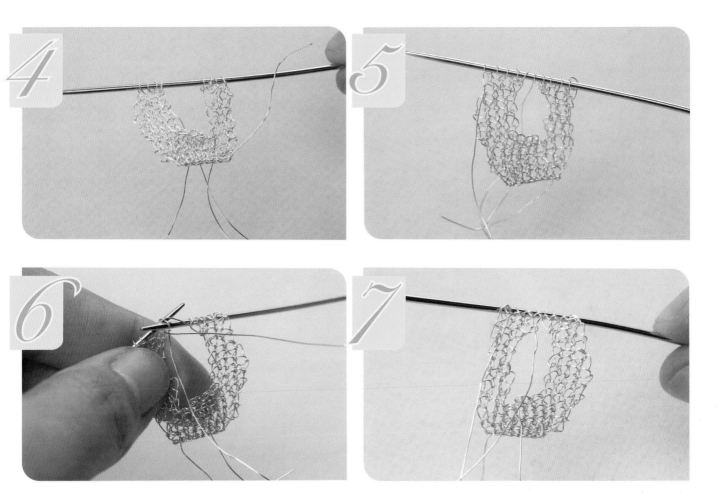

Complete the Earring

Do not cut the wires; use them to wrap the edges. For the inner edges, use the wires that were dropped at the closing of the gaps. If using soldered ear wires, you will need to wrap through the ear wire in order to continue wrapping around it. Once wrapped, cut the wires, tuck in ends with tweezers and place a bead of epoxy to seal.

Cut 4 lengths of wire about 1" (2.5cm) long. Thread a wire through the hole drilled in one of the peridot beads. Leave one end longer than the other and cross them. Holding on to the bead, twist the wires a few times and cut the shorter end. Now thread the wire through the stitch at the very top of the triangular gap and pass the wire over the edge of the wrapped inside gap. Close the loop, making sure it's not too tight so the bead can dangle and wrap around the wire twist on top of the bead (as outlined on page 33). Cut the wire, tuck and secure with an epoxy bead.

Repeat the same process, but this time thread through an iolite teardrop instead. Loop the bead through the space between the fourth and fifth cast-on stitches and wrap the wire around the twist. Cut and secure.

Repeat the process and attach the 2 remaining stones to the other earring.

73

Tip *If you are designing your own knitted piece and you want to decrease stitches, you should try to do so near the beginning of the row—as shown in this piece—because there is less tension on the wire and it is therefore more comfortable. Doing so also avoids twists, which could put much pressure on the wire and break it.*

Viking knitting transforms the common hoop into a sleek and modern piece that is also lightweight. Wire is woven around hexagonal wrenches and then pulled through a drawplate, producing a tube that resembles traditional I-cord. A sturdy, curved wire threaded through the center of each tube then turns them into hoops.

VIKING HOOPS

Materials

30-gauge Argentium or sterling silver soft round wire (about 18' [549cm]) divided into 2 9' (274cm) lengths

21-gauge Argentium or sterling silver hard round wire (about 8 ⅝" [22cm]) divided into 2 4 ⁵⁄₁₆" (11cm) lengths

⅛" (3.2mm), ⁹⁄₆₄" (3.6mm), ⁵⁄₃₂" (4mm), ³⁄₁₆" (4.8mm), ⁷⁄₃₂" (5.6mm), and ¹³⁄₆₄" (5.2mm) hexagonal wrenches

small C-clamp

vise grip

wooden drawplate

needle- or round-nose pliers

wire cutters

clear epoxy or jeweler's cement

needle files

toothpick or pin (for placement of epoxy)

jeweler's tweezers

Pattern

Cast on 7 stitches as outlined for Viking knitting on page 24; mark 1st loop. K4 rows using the ⅛" (3.2mm) hex wrench (**Figures 1** and **2** on page 76). K2 rows using the ⁹⁄₆₄" (3.6mm) hex wrench. K10 rows using the ⁵⁄₃₂" (4mm) hex wrench. Tie a scrap piece of string or wire to the beginning end of the piece in progress and twist it together with the rest of the ends and the marker wire. Remove the piece in progress from the wrench (**Figure 3** on page 77). Thread the twisted end through the ¹³⁄₆₄" (5mm) hole in the drawplate as shown on page 77 (**Figure 4**). Firmly but gently pull the work through the ⅛" (3.2mm) hole in the drawplate. K10 rows using the ³⁄₁₆" (4.8mm) hex wrench. K3 rows using the ⁷⁄₃₂" (5.6mm) hex wrench. K10 rows using the ³⁄₁₆" (4.8mm) hex wrench. Pull through the ¹³⁄₆₄" (5.2mm) hole in the drawplate. K10 rows using the ⁵⁄₃₂" (4mm) hex wrench. K2 rows using the ⁹⁄₆₄" (3.6mm) hex wrench. K4 rows using the ⅛" (3.2mm) hex wrench. Bind off. Pull the last 16 rows through the ⅛" (3.2mm) hole in the drawplate, being careful not to pull the middle 23 rows, in order to keep the "swollen" look.

Completing the Earrings

Continue threading the last stitches through smaller and smaller holes in the drawplate until you can't fit it through any more—about ⅛" (3.2mm). (The smaller it gets, the harder it is to pull, so you may need to use pliers to assist you [**Figure 5**]. If the wire breaks, don't sweat it—that's why you are using the scrap wire tied to the end. Simply tie another piece in its place to assist you in pulling until the piece passes through the smallest hole.)

With the tweezers, remove the flower petal loops—made at the beginning—from each earring. Cut 2 pieces of 21-gauge sterling silver hard wire to a length of about 4⁵⁄₁₆" (11cm). File to remove burrs. Thread one of the wires through each knitted earring (**Figure 6**).

Use needle-nose pliers to form one end of each wire into a tiny hook about ½" (1cm) from the end of the knitted hoop. This will be the portion that goes through the earlobe, and the hook will be used to close the earring. File the end of the hook round and smooth. Use the needle-nose pliers to form the other end of each wire into a sideways loop to serve as a clasp (**Figure 7**).

Wrap the wire end from each knitted piece through the wire hoop or clasp at the back of each earring and securely around the earring itself to create a wire-wrapped coil of about ¼" (6.4mm). At the other end, leave the ½" (1cm) of wire bare and begin sewing the other wire end from the knitted hoop through the knitting (**Figure 8**). Wrap the remaining wire around the 21-gauge wire to secure it in place. Make sure you leave enough space at the top unwrapped so it can accommodate the earlobe. Finish by covering the edge of the hoop with about ⅛" (3.2mm) of wire wrapping. Trim the ends and secure them with a dab of clear epoxy.

Tip *If the knitting covers too much of the 21-gauge wire, you can always make the wrapping smaller (and ultimately, the fit better, by giving it more space for the earlobe), by taking out stitches from the ends of the knit piece. Make sure that this is done evenly on both sides and that once the desired amount of rows is unbound, that it is done equally on the other hoop.*

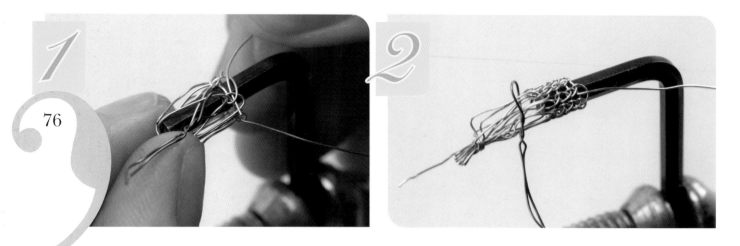

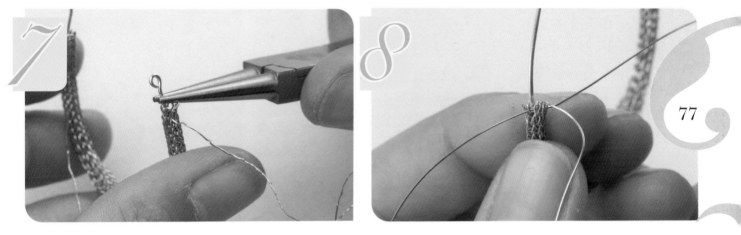

BRACELETS

Because bracelets do not have size or weight restrictions the way rings and earrings do, they can be the perfect candidates for experimentation.

Delicate pieces are given substance by using bold colors, and simple Viking-knit cords become a statement piece when coiled. Ribbons and cords offer the perfect way to customize the size of a bracelet while adding style; as luxurious silk ribbon peeks through metal lace, the already rugged and industrial *Frame Cuff* design (see page 82) is made more so by the addition of another industrial material: rubber.

Because bracelets can be wider, I had more freedom with the patina, so I tried several effects. I approached blank spaces like a canvas on which I painted bold, contrasting designs. But then I also gave a rich, textured depth to knitted cables.

Whether they are thin and dangly or bold and wide, the bracelets in this book showcase new boundaries in the knitted work.

CORAL BRACELET

Materials

set of US 0000 (1.25mm) straight knitting needles

30-gauge Argentium or sterling silver soft round wire (about 18' [549cm]) divided into 4 4' [122cm] lengths and 2 1' (30.5cm) long pieces

1 5mm (.2") 18-gauge Argentium or sterling silver jump ring, soldered closed (you can make your own with 18-gauge wire, making sure the outer diameter is 5mm [.2"])

1 18-gauge Argentium or sterling silver hook clasp about $\frac{2}{5}$" × $\frac{1}{5}$" (10mm × 5mm)

32 red irregular and slightly flattened coral branches, center drilled, about 7mm ($\frac{7}{25}$") long (or similar)

3 lengths of 1.75mm (.07") round cable chain about $\frac{3}{16}$" (4.8mm) each (about 3 links)

needle- or round-nose pliers, if making your own findings

wire cutters

clear epoxy or jeweler's cement

toothpick or pin (for placement of epoxy)

jeweler's tweezers

80

The small, linked, floating islands of algae and foam often found drifting at sea were the inspiration for this piece, but with brighter colors. The irregular shape of the coral beads mimic that of the organic links on which they are knit, and the tiny chain that holds them together becomes invisible against the skin, allowing the links to float. In keeping with this look, and understanding that the shape of each bead will be different, the design allows you to add them to whichever stitch allows for a better fit in that particular row.

Pattern

Make 4 for a bracelet measuring about 6" (15cm) (without clasp). If more length is desired, add another link.

Cast on 3 sts.

Row 1: K3.

Row 2: P1, add bead while purling the next st, p1.

Row 3: Kfb, k2 = 4.

Row 4: P4, adding bead.

Row 5: K3, kfb = 5.

Row 6: P5, adding bead.

Row 7: K5.

Row 8: P5, adding bead.

Row 9: K5.

Row 10: P5, adding bead.

Row 11: K5.

Row 12: P5, adding bead.

Row 13: K5.

Row 14: P5, adding bead.

Row 15: K5.

Row 16: P2tog, p3 = 4.

Row 17: K4.

Row 18: P2, p2tog, adding bead = 3.

Row 19: K3.

Bind off.

Wrap all pieces with the leftover wire. Cut the wire close to the wrapping and tuck in with the tweezers. Place a drop of epoxy with a toothpick to secure. Place a knit piece on your thumb, beaded side up, and press gently against your fingers to create a slight dome.

Assemble the Bracelet

Slide a foot-long piece of 30-gauge wire into a 1½"–2" (4cm–5cm) length of chain and begin tying a loop to secure it (**Figure 1**). Slide the remaining wire into the center loop of the side of one of the links (**Figure 2**), crossing the wire over itself to position the chain flush with the edge of the link. Complete the loop to secure it in place (**Figure 3**). Connect the other end of the chain to a second link using the same process (**Figure 4**).

Repeat until all links are connected. The same process is also used to add a clasp to one end and a jump ring to the other. Once assembled, twist the loops so the links all face the same direction.

81

A complementary piece to the *Frame Ring* (page 50), this cuff inverts the colors. In this case, the sheet metal is textured and patinated, while the silver remains white for the knitted portion. Instead of a clasp, I continued this piece's modern, industrial look by using a piece of black rubber tied in an adjustable manner.

FRAME CUFF

Pattern

Cast on 3 sts.

Rows 1, 3, 5, 7, 9, 11, 13, 15, 17 and 19: K3.

Rows 2, 4, 6, 8, 10, 12, 14, 16 and 18: P3.

Do not bind off.

Materials

set of US 0000 (1.25mm) straight knitting needles

30-gauge Argentium or sterling silver soft round wire (about 4' [122cm])

jeweler's saw

small rubber, nylon or rawhide mallet

22-gauge sterling silver sheet (½" [1cm] wide and 1¾" [4.4cm] long)

12" (30cm) length of 2mm (.08") black rubber cord

awl for marking

hand drill

no. 77 drill bit

³⁄₃₂" (2.4mm) drill bit

wire cutters

liver of sulfur or other darkening agent, dissolved according to manufacturer's instructions

2 fine-tip soft artist's brushes (size 2/0 or smaller)

Butcher's wax, paint wax or cold wax painting medium

clear epoxy or jeweler's cement

toothpick or pin (for placement of epoxy)

jeweler's tweezers

polishing cloth and rouge (if cloth does not already contain compound)

needle files

fine-grit sanding pad

sandpaper (very fine) or steel wool

steel burnisher

scouring pad

ruler

straightedge

paper towels

83

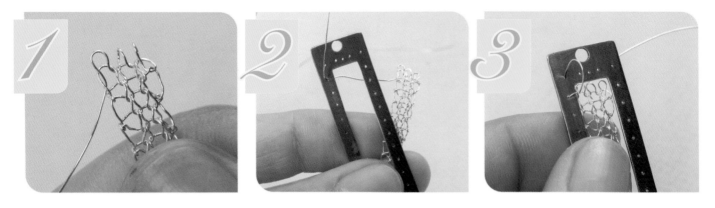

Create Frame

If you have not already, cut your sheet metal to 1¾" × ½" (4.4cm × 1cm) following the instructions as outlined on page 37. Don't forget to file all the edges and corners smooth so they won't catch on anything or scratch your skin. Use a ruler and an awl to mark a centered ¼" × 1¼" (6.4mm × 3.2cm) inner opening as outlined on page 37.

Remove the inner opening as outlined on page 37, taking care to track the blade just inside the marks; you can always file away any excess later.

Once the sheet is cut and filed, measure ¹⁄₁₆" (1.6mm) diagonally from an inside corner and make a mark with an awl. Repeat on the other 3 corners. Then make 10 marks along both 1¼" (3.2cm) lengths of the cutout (about ⅛" [3.2mm] apart), making sure they are ¹⁄₁₆" (1.6mm) from the inner edge. Finally, make 3 marks along the ¼" (6.4mm) sides of the cutout, spacing them evenly, about ¹⁄₁₆" (1.6mm) from each other. Remain ¹⁄₁₆" (1.6mm) from the cutout edge.

With a hand drill and a no. 77 drill bit, carefully drill holes at the marks. For the larger holes, measure and make a mark ¹⁄₁₆" (1.6mm) from the outer side edges of the sheet metal and ¼" (6.4mm) from the top and bottom. Drill into the 2 marks with a ³⁄₃₂" (2.4mm) drill bit. Burnish to remove burrs.

Once your piece is cut, filed and drilled, use a coarse scouring pad to remove any marks made on the surface of the metal piece (as outlined on page 39). Switch to a fine-grit sanding pad and continue distressing and texturing the surface. Here I'm using a 30/40-micron (or about 340/280-grit) double-sided sanding pad, starting with the rougher 40 micron (280 grit) and then finishing with the 30 micron (340 grit) to make sure the surface will pick up the patina nicely in the following steps. Polish the other side of the piece (the underside) with a polishing cloth.

After sanding, drop the piece in a diluted solution of liver of sulfur, following the manufacturer's instructions, as outlined on page 40. Leave the piece in the solution until the desired patina effect is achieved; for the look shown here, I left it in about 5–10 minutes. Then remove the piece and rinse it with water to remove any excess liver of sulfur, which is toxic. Dry it completely with paper towels.

Use your fingers to coat the distressed side of the piece with wax to ensure the effect of the patina does not rub off on your skin. Work a thick coat of the wax into the surface and rub away any excess.

Because the underside of the piece was not distressed, the patina can be more easily removed so it will not rub off on your skin. Simply rub it with the polishing cloth to reveal the shiny metal beneath.

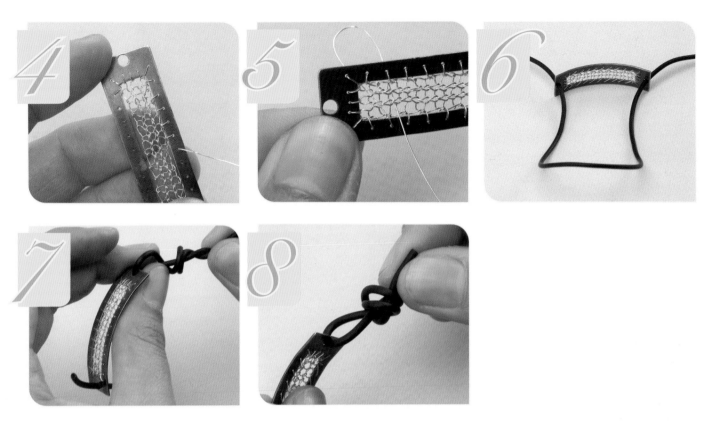

Attach Knitting to Frame

Once you finish the last row of knitting, slide it off the needle without binding off and carefully straighten the loops with tweezers or pliers so they lie flat like the others below them (**Figure 1**).

Temporarily pull the wire end through the cast-on edge and then through the center hole in one side of the piece just to help hold it as you use your fingers to manipulate the rest of the knitting into place inside the frame, knit side up. Thread the working-wire end up through the hole on its corresponding side at the other end of the piece (**Figure 2**).

Working in a clockwise direction so as not to let the corner stitch slip off, thread the wire down through the adjacent hole in the knitting (**Figure 3**) and then up through the next hole in the frame.

Continue in this manner around the perimeter of the frame, pulling each stitch taut to attach the knitted piece securely to the sheet metal (**Figure 4**).

When you reach the end, sew it through an adjacent knitted stitch to secure it (**Figure 5**), trim the excess wire and use pliers to tuck in the end. Trim and tuck the other wire end as well. Bend the piece with your fingers to make it slightly convex.

Assemble the Bracelet

Cut a 12" (30cm) length of 2mm (.08") black rubber cord. Thread it through each end of the metal piece (the ³⁄₃₂" [2.4mm] holes) from the bottom up (**Figure 6**), leaving about 3" (7.6cm) of cord poking through each end.

Begin tying an adjustable knot in one end by wrapping the cord around itself twice (**Figure 7**). Finish the knot by passing it over the wraps to the top of the 2 wraps you made in the previous step and pulling it down through the wraps tightly (**Figure 8**). Repeat at the other end and adjust the length to fit your wrist as necessary.

One of the most unusual bracelets, this cuff is inspired by the geometric shapes of 1960s go-go designs but retains a sleek, contemporary look. I simply cut out the circles from cardboard and traced them directly onto the knitted mesh. I painted wax around those circles and applied patina to their bare interiors. Once the color developed, I rinsed off the patina and removed the wax from around the circles. I applied wax again as a protective coating, but this time only to the interiors of the now-black circles, using a very soft paintbrush to avoid removing the patina.

PAINTED CUFF

Materials

set of US 0000 (1.25mm) straight knitting needles

30-gauge Argentium or sterling silver wire (about 45' [1372cm])

3 5mm (.2") 18-gauge Argentium or sterling silver jump rings, soldered closed (you can make your own out of 18-gauge wire, making sure the outer diameter is 5mm [.2"])

3 18-gauge Argentium or sterling silver hook clasps about ⅜" (10mm) long and ⅕" (5mm) wide

nylon-covered coiling flat jaw pliers (if making your own findings)

wire cutters

liver of sulfur or other darkening agent, dissolved according to the manufacturer's instructions

2 fine-tip soft artist's brushes (size 2/0 or smaller)

small, very soft paintbrush (makeup brushes work well)

Butcher's wax, paint wax or cold wax painting medium

clear epoxy or jeweler's cement

toothpick or pin (for placement of epoxy)

jeweler's tweezers

polishing cloth and rouge (if cloth does not already contain compound)

ruler

paper towels

Pattern

Cast on 16 sts.

Pull needle out carefully and add jump rings to cast-on row between the first 2 stitches, then between the 8th and 9th stitches, and finally between the last 2 stitches. Thread the needle back in and continue knitting (as outlined on page 29).

Row 1: K16, incorporating jump rings.

Rows 2–100: P16 for all even rows.

Rows 3–99: K16 for all odd rows.

Add clasps while binding off if soldered closed. Place the first clasp after binding off the first stitch, the second clasp after binding off the 8th stitch and the last clasp after binding off the 15th stitch (as outlined on page 31). Bind off the last stitch and cut the wire, leaving it about ½" (1cm) long.

Add Patina Design

Pin the bracelet flat on a scrap piece of cardboard or foam core and use a ruler and a pencil to mark 3 evenly spaced spots where the 3 circles of the design will go. Make a circular template with cardboard or paper that has a diameter of a little bit less than 1" (2.5cm). Using a water-soluble marker or piece of chalk, draw an axis on the circle. Place the circle into position on the bracelet next to the first mark and lightly mark the bracelet with the dots of the axis (**Figure 1**). Repeat for the other 2 marks.

Use a paintbrush to brush wax carefully over all areas of the bracelet except for the circles, dabbing it into the crevices. This will act as a mask for the patina. For precision, you may want to place the circle template back into place as you paint around each one (**Figure 2**).

Use a different paintbrush to paint diluted liver of sulfur inside each of the circles to give the unwaxed area a nice patina (**Figure 3**). Gently work it into all the twists of the knitted wire with the brush. If you wait a few minutes, you can see the patina developing.

In **Figure 4**, you can see how the circles painted first are darker than the one that was painted last.

When you've created an effect you like, rinse the piece under water. Use a super-soft paintbrush or makeup brush to coat the patinated areas with wax to prevent the patina from coming off on your skin (**Figure 5**).

Rub the entire bracelet with a polishing cloth to remove the excess wax (**Figure 6**). If the patina stained any areas outside the circles, you can polish that off as well. When you start feeling a bit of resistance as you rub, you'll know the wax has been removed.

Wire wrap the perimeter of the entire bracelet, making sure that when you get to either a jump ring or a clasp, you pass the wire through the findings. Cut the remaining wire close to the edge, tuck in with tweezers and place a dab of epoxy at the end to seal.

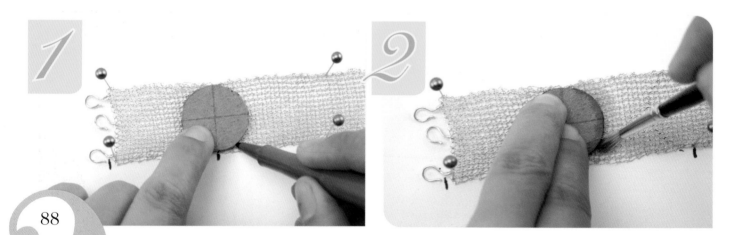

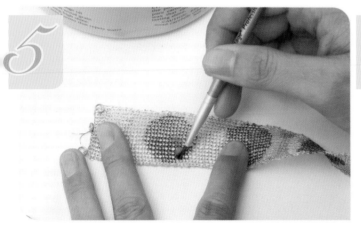

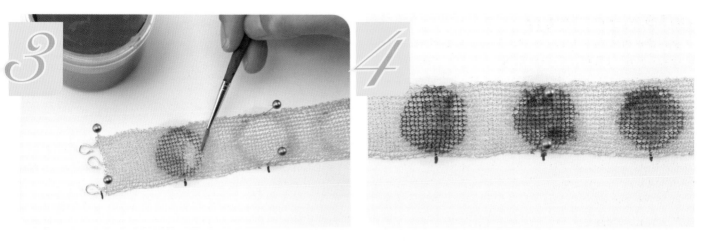

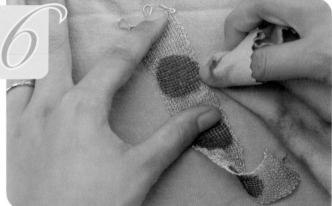

VIKING CUFF

I drew inspiration from Viking imagery for this bracelet's design, as well as from a photo of a family of snakes. Once coiled, the cords repeat a pattern of colors, bringing to mind ancient designs. By changing the wrench sizes while knitting, I achieved different thicknesses in the tubes, which allowed me to stuff some wider spaces with iridescent freshwater pearls.

Materials

1 spool of 28-gauge soft round gold-colored copper wire (about 15 yards [13.5m])

1 spool of 28-gauge soft round sterling silver or silver-colored copper wire (about 15 yards [13.5m])

1 spool of 28-gauge soft round bronze-colored copper wire (about 15 yards [13.5m])

%4" (3.6mm), ⁵⁄₃₂" (4mm), ³⁄₁₆" (4.6mm), ⁷⁄₆₄" (2.8mm), ⁷⁄₃₂" (5.6mm) and ¼" (6.4mm) hexagonal wrenches

1 18-gauge Argentium or sterling silver hook clasp about ⅖" × ⅕" (10mm × 5mm) (or about 1" [2.5cm] 18-gauge wire to make it yourself)

1 5mm (.2") 18-gauge Argentium or sterling silver jump ring, soldered closed (you can make your own out of 18-gauge wire, making sure the outer diameter is 5mm [.2"])

small C-clamp

vise grip

wooden drawplate

12 bronze rice-shaped freshwater pearls (3–3.5mm [³⁄₂₅"–⁷⁄₅₀"] long)

needle- or round-nose pliers

wire cutters

clear epoxy or jeweler's cement

toothpick or pin (for placement of epoxy)

jeweler's tweezers

a few pieces of scrap wire

Pattern

See page 24 for more on the Viking knitting technique.

Silver cord: Cast on 7 sts using the Viking knitting technique; mark 1st loop. K22 rows using the 5⁄32" (4mm) hex wrench. K15 rows using the 3⁄16" (4.8mm) hex wrench. Tie a scrap piece of string or wire to the beginning end of the piece in progress and twist it together with the rest of the ends and the marker wire (do this for each cord). Remove the piece in progress from the wrench. Thread the twisted end through the 3⁄16" (4.8mm) hole in the drawplate as outlined on page 27. Firmly but gently, keep pulling the work through decreasing holes until it can go through the 7⁄64" (2.8mm) hole in the drawplate.

K14 rows using the 3⁄16" (4.8mm) hex wrench. Fill new rows with pearls (should be able to fit 2 to 3) and then put the knitting back on the wrench. K15 rows using the 3⁄16" (4.7mm) hex wrench. K27 using the 5⁄32" (3.9mm) hex wrench. Bind off by threading the wire through the loops so they don't unravel. Pull the last 42 rows through the 7⁄64" (2.8mm) hole in the drawplate.

Gold cord: Cast on 7 sts; mark 1st loop. K24 rows using the 5⁄32" (4mm) hex wrench. Pull work through 7⁄64" (2.8mm) hole. K4 rows using the 3⁄16" (4.8mm) hex wrench. K6 rows using the 5⁄32" (4mm) hex wrench. Fill last 10 rows with pearls (about 3). K2 rows using the 9⁄64" (3.6mm) hex wrench. K2 rows using the 3⁄16" (4.8mm) hex wrench. K2 rows using the 7⁄32" (5.6mm) hex wrench. Pinch the last 6 rows to secure pearls. K2 rows using the 1⁄4" (6.4mm) hex wrench. K2 rows using the 3⁄16" (4.8mm) hex wrench. Fill the last 4 rows with pearls (about 2). K48 rows using the 5⁄32" (4mm) hex wrench. Bind off. Pull the last 48 rows through 7⁄64" (2.8mm) hole.

Bronze cord: Cast on 6 sts; mark 1st loop. K16 rows using the 9⁄64" (3.6mm) hex wrench. K14 rows using the 5⁄32" (4mm) hex wrench. Pull the last 30 rows through 7⁄64" (2.8mm) hole. K5 rows using the 7⁄32" (5.6mm) hex wrench. Fill the last 5 rows with pearls (2 to 3). K4 rows using the 5⁄32" (4mm) hex wrench. K2 rows using the 9⁄64" (3.6mm) hex wrench. Pinch the last 6 rows to secure pearls. K8 rows using the 7⁄32" (5.6mm) hex wrench. Fill the 8 new rows with pearls. K14 rows using the 5⁄32" (4mm) hex wrench. K16 rows using the 9⁄64" (3.6mm) hex wrench. Bind off. Pull the last 30 rows through 7⁄64" (2.8mm) hole.

Assemble the Bracelet

Remove the flower-petal loops containing the wire marker made at the beginning of each cord, and once all the stitches are the same size, pull the wire tight to close the tube. Cut the wire and tuck in with tweezers. Place a drop of epoxy to seal, and repeat the process for the other 2 cords.

Cut 2 lengths of the silver wire about 6" (15cm) long each and thread one through the stitches at the opposite end of the silver cord, leaving 3" (7.6cm) of wire on either side of the cord. Making sure the stitches face the same direction, thread the same wire through the opposing stitches at the ends of both the gold and bronze cords. Pull the two ends of the wire together and twist twice to tighten all the cords together.

Now, with all 3 cords attached, grab their loose ends and twist them around each other, still holding the connected end. Keep turning until the twists no longer unravel when the connected end is released. Sew the other 6" (15cm) length of silver wire halfway through stitches in the cord (which is now made up of 3 different cords) until all 3 ends are secure. Now sew the 2 ends of the 6" (15cm) length into the center and pull together to tighten. Twist twice.

The remaining wire holding the cord ends together will serve to form loops to attach the clasp and jump ring.

Grab either end and cross the wires at that end over each other (see *Wrapping a Loop* on page 33). In this case there will be 4 wires instead of 2, so they will be doubled up for strength. Twist the wires together and clip the two wires close to the twist. Now thread the remaining two wires through the jump ring and pull the wires over the twist to close and finally wrap the twist. Cut the wires close to the wraps and tuck in the ends with tweezers. Seal with a drop of epoxy.

Repeat the same process with the wires at the other end, this time adding the clasp instead of the jump ring. Repeat for the other 2 cords.

For this piece, I was inspired by the rich texture of traditional Aran wool designs. However, I gave those designs a more modern edge by working them in a patinated metal. Although the more brittle nature of metal wire somewhat limits the range of traditional knitting techniques you can use, cabling can be achieved without causing too much stress on the material. At first, the knitting appears to be a tangled mess, but when patina is applied to the recesses inside and around the cables, their dense, velvety texture really shines through.

PATINATED SILVER CABLE CUFF

Materials

set of US 0000 (1.25mm) straight knitting needles

safety pin or paper clip (used as a cable needle)

30-gauge fine or sterling silver soft round wire (about 42' [1280cm])

12" (30cm) length of 2mm (.08") black rubber cord

wire cutters

liver of sulfur or other darkening agent, dissolved according to manufacturer's instructions

2 fine-tip soft artist's brushes (size 2/0 or smaller)

small, very soft brush (makeup brushes work well)

Butcher's wax, paint wax or cold wax painting medium

clear epoxy or jeweler's cement

toothpick or pin (for placement of epoxy)

jeweler's tweezers

polishing cloth and rouge (if cloth does not already contain compound)

Pattern

Repeat pattern twice for proper length.

Cast on 20 sts.

Rows 1 (RS) and 5: P4, c4f, p4, c4f, p4.

Rows 2, 4, 6 and 24: K4, p4, k4, p4, k4.

Row 3: P4, k4, p4, k4, p4.

Row 7: P2, [t4b, t4f] twice, p2.

Rows 8, 10, 12, 14, 16, 18, 20 and 22: K2, p2, k4, p4, k4, p2, k2.

Rows 9, 13, 17 and 21: P2, k2, p4, c4f, p4, k2, p2.

Row 11, 15, 19: P2, k2, p4, k4, p4, k2, p2.

Row 23: P2, [t4f, t4b] twice, p2.

Bind off.

After the pattern is repeated, use the remaining wire to wrap all edges of the knit piece. Cut the end close to the wrapping and tuck in the end with tweezers.

Knitting Abbreviations

Although most of the piece is plain Stockinette, there are a few variations in the pattern (photos on pages 94–95):

c4f: sl next 2 st(s) to cable needle (cn) and hold in front, k2 from left needle (see **Figure 1**), k2 from cn (see **Figure 2**).

t4b: sl next 2 st(s) to cn and hold in back (see Figure 3), k2 from left needle (see **Figure 4**), p2 from cn (see **Figure 5**).

t4f: sl next 2 st(s) to cn and hold in front, p2 from left needle (see **Figure 6**), k2 from cn (see **Figure 7**).

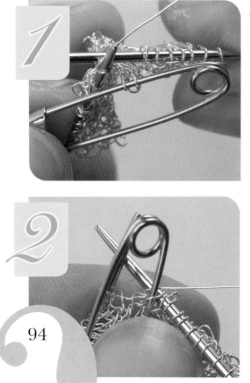

Assemble the Cuff

Dip one of the brushes into the wax and brush the raised braids in the knitting to protect them from oxidation while the patina is applied. With the other brush, apply the liver of sulfur into the concave portions of the piece as well as the wrapped edges. Make sure to dab the solution into the stitches to ensure thorough coverage. Once the piece has taken on a deep color, rinse the entire piece in water.

With a soft brush, apply a thin coating of wax onto the patinated areas to seal the finish. Remove any excess with a polishing cloth, being careful to leave the patina intact. Now polish the raised cable design until shiny and white. Finally, polish the underside of the piece until the patina stops rubbing off on the cloth, seal with wax and rub the excess one more time.

Thread the 12" (30cm) rubber cord through the opening between the 10th and 11th stitches at each end of the knit piece from the bottom up and pull so that each end has an equal amount of rubber cord at the ends (it will essentially look like a very large running stitch). To wear the cuff, the knitting alone will be on top of your wrist, while the two loose ends will pull back in toward the center to be tied into a bow, in order to tighten the rubber cord.

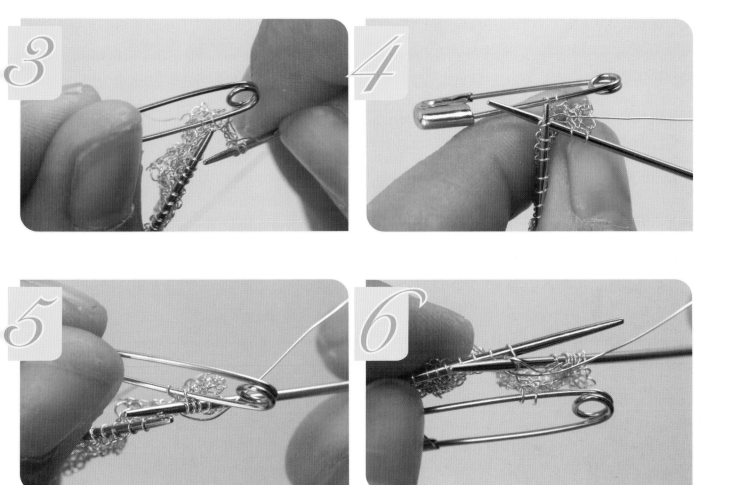

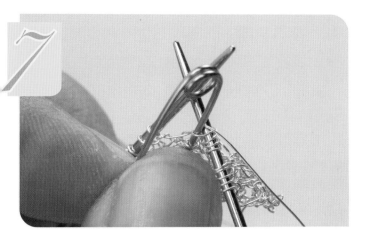

Reminiscent of Victorian times, this simple and organic bracelet is incredibly light, comfortable and feminine. The large gap in the center of the Stockinette panel allows for the dark, silk ribbon to show through. Replacing a clasp with a pretty bow, I sewed this ribbon on with a simple running stitch, again showcasing the versatility of knitted metal wire.

GREEN RIBBON CUFF

Materials

set of US 0000 (1.25mm) straight knitting needles

30-gauge Argentium or sterling silver soft round wire (about 11.5' [351cm]) cut into 2 5' (152cm) pieces for the knitting and wrapping and 1 18" (46cm) piece for the sewing

wire cutters

clear epoxy or jeweler's cement

clear nail polish

toothpick or pin (for placement of epoxy)

jeweler's tweezers

⅗" (15mm) wide silk ribbon (forest green is shown), enough to fit around your wrist and tie (18½" [47cm] as shown here)

ruler

chalk

sewing needle (optional)

Like the *Peridot and Iolite Earrings* (page 70), this pattern also creates a gap by adding a second wire, binding off a section in the middle of the row, and continuing to knit two patterns simultaneously, at times decreasing and increasing stitches to vary the width of the gap. To close the gap, one of the wires is dropped, and the other is used to continue the pattern. Refer to page 35 for more on creating gaps.

Pattern

Cast on 5 sts.

Row 1: K5.

Row 2: P5.

Row 3: Kfb, k3, kfb = 7.

Row 4: P7.

Row 5: Kfb, k6 = 8.

Row 6: P8.

Row 7: K3, add new wire (W2), BO1, k4 = 7.

Row 8: P4 with W2; p2tog, p1 with original wire (W1) = 6.

Row 9: K2 with W1; k2tog, k2 with W2 = 5.

Row 10: P3 with W2; p2 with W1.

Row 11: K2 with W1; k2, kfb with W2 = 6.

Row 12: P2, p2tog with W2; p2 with W1 = 5.

Row 13: K1, kfb with W1; k3 with W2 = 6.

Row 14: P3 with W2; p3 with W1.

Row 15: K3 with W1; kfb, k2 with W2 = 7.

Row 16: P4 with W2; p3 with W1.

Row 17: K3 with W1; k4 with W2.

Row 18: P4 with W2; p2tog, p1 with W1 = 6.

Row 19: K2 with W1; k4 with W2.

Row 20: P4 with W2; p2 with W1.

Row 21: K2 with W1; k2tog, k2 with W2 = 5.

Row 22: P3 with W2; p2 with W1.

Row 23: K1, kfb with W1; k3 with W2 = 6.

Row 24: P3 with W2; p3 with W1.

Row 25: K2, kfb with W1; k3 with W2 = 7.

Row 26: P3 with W2; p4 with W1.

Row 27: K4 with W1; kfb, k2 with W2 = 8.

Row 28: P8 with W2, dropping W1.

Row 29: K8.

Row 30: P2tog, p6 = 7.

Row 31: K2tog, k5 = 6.

Row 32: P2tog, p4 = 5.

Row 33: K2tog, k3 = 4.

Row 34: P4.

Bind off.

Do not cut the wires; use them to wrap the edges. Wire wrap all the edges of the knitted piece, including the outer perimeter as well as the center opening. For the inner edges, use the wires that were dropped at the closing of the gaps.

Sew Knitted Piece to Cuff

Cut the ends of the ribbon into decorative *V* shapes. Coat the ends lightly with a bit of clear nail polish to keep them from fraying. Measure the center of the ribbon and mark it with chalk. Center the knitted piece over the mark. Start in the center, near the edge, and thread the 18" (46cm) length of wire down through the knitted piece and the ribbon (**Figure 1**). Leave a wire tail about 1" (2.5cm) long as you work.

Start with a big running stitch to help hold the piece in place as you work. Then start working a running stitch around the perimeter, stitching the knitting to the ribbon (**Figures 2** and **3**). To avoid creasing the ribbon, be sure to stitch over the arms of the knitted stitches, rather than over the wire-wrapped perimeter of the knitted piece.

Once you've established a line of stitching to the end of that edge, go back and secure the wire end you started with, from the right side of the bracelet, by tying it in a knot through the ribbon and over the arm of a knitted stitch (**Figure 4**). Trim the excess wire and tuck in the end. Seal with a drop of epoxy, being careful not to get it onto the ribbon, as it darkens the fabric.

Continue stitching around the entire perimeter of the knitted piece. When you reach the end, secure the wire end.

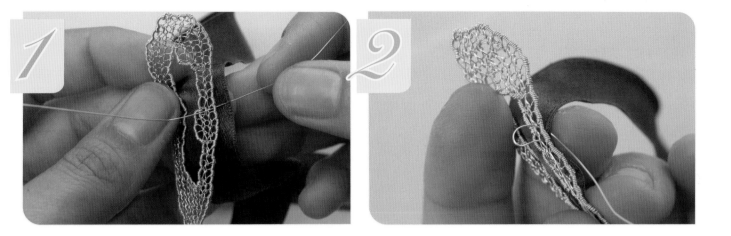

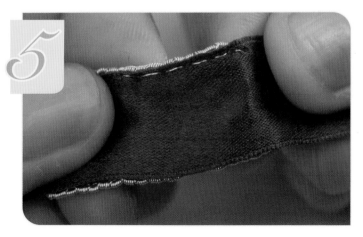

Tip If you're having a hard time threading the wire through the ribbon, thread the wire through a needle for easier stitching.

Subtle in its complexity, this bracelet combines almost all the techniques into one piece. Small panels of Stockinette are sewn onto little sheet-metal frames. Although the piece is wide, it remains delicate due to the fact that I constructed it from several Viking-knit cables, as opposed to one solid piece. All these components make this bracelet rich in texture, but the small size of each of its parts make it graceful.

MIXED-LINK BRACELET

Materials

set of US 0000 (1.25mm) straight knitting needles

3 pieces of 30-gauge Argentium or sterling silver soft round wire (about 24" [61cm] each) for framed knitting

6 pieces of 30-gauge Argentium or sterling silver soft round wire (about 12" [30cm] each) for small Viking-knit cords

6 pieces of 30-gauge Argentium or sterling silver soft round wire (about 36" [91cm] each) for large Viking-knit cords

jeweler's saw (I use a size 4)

22-gauge sterling silver sheet about ¾" × 1¼" (1.9cm × 3.2cm) cut into 3 pieces measuring ¾" × 5⁄16" (1.9cm × 8mm) for frames and 2 pieces measuring ¾" × 5⁄32" (1.9cm × 4mm) for the ends of the bracelet

¾" (1.9cm) length of 21-gauge Argentium or sterling silver hard round wire for clasp

1 23-gauge Argentium or sterling silver jump ring soldered closed (4mm [.16"])

awl for marking

hand drill

no. 77 drill bit

no. 70 for clasp

drill bit slightly larger than the saw blades being used (no smaller than a size 60)

small C-clamp

vise grip

wooden drawplate

nylon-covered half-needle-nose pliers (for making clasp)

wire cutters

clear epoxy or jeweler's cement

toothpick or pin (for placement of epoxy)

jeweler's tweezers

polishing cloth and rouge (if cloth does not already contain compound)

needle files

fine-grit sanding pad

sandpaper (very fine) or steel wool

steel burnisher

scouring pad

5⁄64" (3.6mm) and 7⁄64" (2.8mm) hexagonal wrenches

Pattern

Make 3.

Cast on 3 sts.

Rows 1, 3, 5, 7 and 9: K3.

Rows 2, 4, 6 and 8: P3.

Bind off.

Do not cut the wire, as it will be used to sew onto frames.

For the creation of the Viking-knit cords, refer to page 24 for more on this technique.

Make 6 shorter cords:

Cast on 4 sts using the Viking knitting technique; mark 1st loop. K7 rows using the 5⁄64" (3.6mm) hex wrench. Bind off. Pull through the 7⁄64" (2.8mm) hole in the drawplate. Grab both ends with your fingers and pull to continue stretching the Viking-knit piece. Do not cut extra wires.

Make 6 longer cords:

Cast on 4 sts using the Viking knitting technique; mark 1st loop. K24 rows using the 5⁄64" (3.6mm) hex wrench. Bind off.

Pull through the 7⁄64" (2.8mm) hole in the drawplate.

Grab both ends with your fingers and continue stretching the Viking-knit piece. Do not cut extra wires.

Prepare the Frames

Cut 3 rectangles (if you have not done so already) ¾" × ⁵⁄₁₆" (1.9cm × 8mm) and 2 rectangles measuring ¾" × ⁵⁄₃₂" (1.9cm × 4mm) out of the 22-gauge sheet metal and file all the edges and corners smooth (see *Working with Sheet Metal* on page 37).

Frame Rectangles

Once the edges of the rectangles have been filed, measure and mark another rectangle ³⁄₁₆" × ⅝" (4.8mm × 16mm) within each piece, starting ¹⁄₁₆" (1.6mm) in from the edges. This should leave a ¹⁄₁₆" (1.6mm) border of metal around the marked center rectangles. With a drill bit slightly larger than your saw blades, drill a hole within the newly marked rectangle. Keeping the blade on the inside of the marks, cut out the rectangle (see *Cutting and Filing a Piece of Sheet Metal* on page 37) and file any excess material off and the edges smooth. Repeat for the other sheet metal pieces.

Lay 1 of the rectangles with its long sides horizontal and mark ¹⁄₃₂" (.8mm) from the top left horizontal edge at the corner and then again ¹⁄₃₂" (.8mm) from the vertical edge. Repeat with the same measurements at the remaining corners so you have 4 marks, 1 at each corner.

Now, with the piece still lying horizontally, measure ⅜" (9.5mm) across the edge (it should be halfway) and make a mark ¹⁄₃₂" (.8mm) in from the edge. From the center mark you just made on the top edge, measure ³⁄₁₆" (4.8mm) to both the left and the right, staying ¹⁄₃₂" (.8mm) from the edge, and mark both measurements with the awl. Along that top edge you should now have 3 center marks and 2 marks at the corners, for a total of 5. Repeat the markings at the opposite edge.

For the remaining lateral edges, measure ⁵⁄₃₂" (4mm) from each side across the edge and mark, ¹⁄₃₂" (.8mm) from the edge. There should now be 3 marks on this smaller edge. Repeat for the opposite edge. Repeat all markings on the other 2 rectangles. With a no. 77 drill bit, carefully drill holes at all the markings. With a burnisher, remove any burrs left from drilling.

Clasp and Jump-Ring Rectangles

Lay one of the smaller rectangles with the ¾" (1.9cm) side horizontal and, like the others, measure and mark ¹⁄₃₂" (.8mm) from both the bottom and left edges on the bottom left corner. Repeat for the bottom right corner. Now measure ⅜" (9.5mm) across that same edge, staying ¹⁄₃₂" (.8mm) from the edge, and mark. You should now have 3 equidistant sections along the bottom.

Across from these marks, on the top edge, measure and mark ⅜" (9.5mm) from the lateral edges and ¹⁄₃₂" (.8mm) from the top edge. Drill all holes on this rectangle with a no. 77 drill bit and remove burrs. Repeat, but instead of drilling the sole mark on the top edge with a no. 77 bit, use a larger no. 70 in order to thread the clasp. Sand the surfaces of the sheet metal pieces until smooth and then polish (as outlined on page 39).

Assemble the Frames

After completing the Stockinette panels (but not binding off), carefully straighten the last stitches with tweezers so they lay flat like the others (as outlined on page 23). See *Frame Cuff* (page 82) for further instruction on sewing knitted panels into sheet-metal frames.

Assemble the Bracelet

Remove the flower-petal loops made at the beginning from each cord, using the tweezers to assist you. Thread the extra wires at each end of the cords through all the loops on each corresponding end and tighten. With the knit side facing up and with the ¾" (1.9cm) side of the rectangle sitting vertically, thread the extra wire of one of the smaller cords down through the middle hole and cross it over and finish tying a loop (as outlined on page 33).

Attach the remaining small cords first to the middle hole on the opposite side and then to the surrounding 4 corner holes, making sure the direction of the stitches on the cords is the same. This center frame piece should now have 6 small cords attached to its perimeter. In the same manner, attach the loose ends of the smaller cords to the sides of the remaining 2 frames (**Figure 1**).

Tie 1 end of each of the longer cords to the 2 outer frames (at the sides opposing those that already have

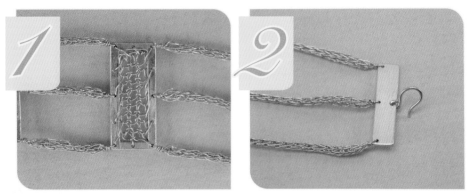

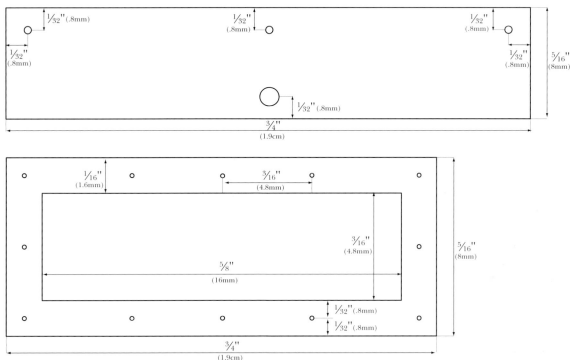

the small cords tied), again making sure the stitches run in the same direction. Once done, the 2 outer frames should now each have 3 longer cords. With the bracelet lying horizontally, the knit sides on the frames up, work to attach first the 3 cords on the left to the rectangle, which will have the jump ring. Attach the cords, as discussed above, to the 3 small holes drilled along the ¾" (1.9cm) edge of the rectangle (the top cord to the top corner hole, middle cord to middle hole, and bottom cord to the bottom corner hole). On the opposite side, thread a small piece of wire (about 1" [2.5cm] long) through the hole and begin tying a loop. Add the jump ring and continue to secure the knot. Repeat the process above, but this time tie the cords on the right side to the 3 holes drilled on the clasp rectangle.

Cut all extra lengths of wire, tuck the ends in with tweezers and seal all with small drops of epoxy.

Add Clasp

Thread the 21-gauge length of wire up through the larger hole on the right end sheet metal piece of the bracelet. Pull up about halfway, and with the tip of the nylon-covered half-needle-nose pliers, make a circle with the end on the knit side of the bracelet large enough to fit the ¹⁄₃₂" (.8mm) edge of the rectangle. Open the circle slightly, pull the wire back down, and once the edge sits comfortably in the loop, close to secure. Now use the pliers to form the rest of the hook clasp by placing the remaining wire between the nylon (on the outside) and the steel (on the inside) and bending the wire around the steel (**Figure 2**).

NECKLACES

Because they are worn directly under your face, necklaces can be crucial when creating a mood or style; they are a direct reflection of personality. Tiny modifications to a design are obvious in a necklace, so details such as chains and gemstones, even a difference in the color of wire, play a major role.

Simple shapes, such as rectangles and squares, can be transformed from a small, quiet silver pendant (see *Mini Tag Pendant*, page 106) to a graphic statement by adding a few stripes (see *Striped Necklace*, page 108) and even to a representational flower by simply curling the corners (see *Lily Necklace*, page 114). Two simple Viking-knit cords, when worn as one terraced piece, become classic and elegant (see *Viking Necklace*, page 112).

Decadent materials such as velvet, silk and gemstones can also be used in a single statement piece (see *Velvet Necklace*, page 110). A sweet butterfly becomes a jeweled specimen with the addition of a few rocks (see *Butterfly Necklace*, page 120), while clusters of turquoise chips, knit into a teardrop, appear to trickle (see *Turquoise Necklace*, page 118).

Arguably the easiest piece to make, this ultrafeminine and delicate pendant looks great worn alone, but if you make more than one, they can be worn as separate, layered pieces hung on different lengths of chain, or as charms on one. This straightforward piece features the simple Stockinette stitch and wire-wrapping techniques...and nothing else.

MINI TAG PENDANT

Materials

set of US 0000 (1.25mm) straight knitting needles

30-gauge Argentium or sterling silver soft round wire (about 36" [91cm])

Argentium or sterling silver 1mm (.04") round cable chain about 17" (43cm) long

23-gauge Argentium or sterling silver jump ring soldered closed (4mm [.16"])

21-gauge Argentium or sterling silver jump ring (5mm [.2"])

23-gauge Argentium or sterling silver hook clasp about ⁵⁄₁₆" × ⁹⁄₅₀" (8mm × 4.5mm)

nylon-covered coiling flat jaw pliers (if making your own findings)

wire cutters

clear epoxy or jeweler's cement

toothpick or pin (for placement of epoxy)

jeweler's tweezers

Pattern

Cast on 5 sts.

Rows 1, 3, 5, 7 and 9: K5.

Rows 2, 4, 6 and 8: P5.

Bind off while adding the 5mm (.2") jump ring, if soldered closed, at the third stitch (as outlined on page 30). Do not cut the extra wire. Wrap the perimeter of the knit piece with the extra wire, passing the wire through the jump ring (if soldered closed and already attached). Once wrapped, cut the wire close to the wrapping, tuck in the end among the wraps with tweezers and place a bead of epoxy with a toothpick to seal.

Assemble the Pendant

If using an open 5mm (.2") jump ring, open the ring and thread through the third stitch on the top row. Close tight with pliers.

Thread a 1" (2.5cm) piece of leftover wire through the last link at one end of the chain and cross to tie a loop (as outlined on page 33), adding the 4mm (.16") jump ring.

Pass the unfinished edge of the chain through the 5mm (.2") jump ring with the knit side up, from right to left, so the jump ring is now on the right side. Again, thread a 1" (2.5cm) piece of wire through the last link of the other side of the chain and, with another loop, attach the clasp.

107

STRIPED NECKLACE

Materials

set of US 0000 (1.25mm) straight knitting needles

30-gauge Argentium or sterling silver wire (about 10' [305cm]) for knitting and wrapping

30-gauge fine or sterling silver wire, darkened and waxed as outlined on page 40 (about 48" [122cm]) for knitting

Argentium or sterling silver 1mm (.04") round cable chain about 19" (48cm) long cut into 2 9¼" (23.5cm) pieces

3 23-gauge Argentium or sterling silver jump rings soldered closed (4mm [.16"])

23-gauge Argentium or sterling silver hook clasp about ⁵⁄₁₆" × ⁹⁄₅₀" (8mm × 4.5mm)

nylon-covered coiling flat jaw pliers (if making your own findings)

wire cutters

liver of sulfur or other darkening agent, dissolved according to manufacturer's instructions

Butcher's wax, paint wax, or cold wax painting medium

clear epoxy or jeweler's cement

toothpick or pin (for placement of epoxy)

jeweler's tweezers

polishing cloth and rouge (if cloth does not already contain compound)

paper towels

While this modern, graphic necklace was designed as a complement to the *Etched Stripe Ring* (page 48), it also looks fresh when worn alone. Like the ring, this piece is knit in Stockinette, changing colors every few rows. The dark wire is patinated and waxed prior to knitting, and its dull surface serves to accentuate the color changes.

Pattern

Cast on 15 sts with patinated silver (PS).

Row 1: K15 with PS.

Row 2: P15 with PS; cut, leaving ½" (1cm) tail.

Row 3: Add sterling silver (SS), drop PS wire, then k15 with SS.

Row 4: P15 with SS; cut, leaving ½" (1cm) tail.

Row 5: Add PS and k15.

Row 6: P15 with PS.

Row 7: K15 with PS.

Row 8: P15 with PS; cut, leaving ½" (1cm) tail.

Row 9: Add SS and k15.

Row 10: P15 with SS; cut, leaving ½" (1cm) tail.

Row 11: Add PS and k15; cut, leaving ½" (1cm) tail.

Row 12: Add SS and p15; cut, leaving ½" (1cm) tail.

Row 13: Add PS and k15.

Row 14: P15 with PS; cut, leaving ½" (1cm) tail.

Row 15: Add SS and k15.

Row 16: P15 with SS.

Row 17: K15 with SS.

Row 18: P15 with SS; cut, leaving ½" (1cm) tail.

Row 19: Add PS and k15; cut, leaving ½" (1cm) tail.

Row 20: Add SS and p15.

Row 21: K15 with SS; cut, leaving ½" (1cm) tail.

Row 22: Add PS and p15.

Row 23: K15 with PS.

Row 24: P15 with PS; cut, leaving ½" (1cm) tail.

Row 25: Add SS and k15.

Row 26: P15 with SS.

Row 27: K15 with SS; cut, leaving ½" (1cm) tail.

Row 28: Add PS and p15.

Row 29: K15 with PS; cut, leaving ½" (1cm) tail.

Row 30: Add SS and p15.

Row 31: K15 with SS.

Row 32: P15 with SS.

Row 33: K15 with SS.

Bind off, adding jump rings after the 1st stitch and before the last stitch (as outlined on page 30).

Do not cut wire. Use the leftover wire to wrap the edges of the piece, taking care to pass the wire through the jump rings as they are soldered closed.

Assemble Necklace

Cut 4 1" (2.5cm) pieces of the leftover Argentium or sterling silver 30-gauge wire. Thread one of the wires through the right jump ring (with the piece knit side up and jump rings at the top) and make half of a loop (as outlined on page 33), adding the last link of 1 of the chains at the end. Repeat for the second jump ring on the necklace with a second piece of chain.

Holding the chain attached to the right side of the necklace (still facing the same way), use another 1" (2.5cm) length of wire to again make another loop and attach the third jump ring to the last link of the loose chain.

Repeat at the other side, adding the clasp instead.

VELVET NECKLACE

Photographs of caves with glittering stalactites inspired this opulent and eclectic necklace. I sewed black silk velvet into the gap in the knitted piece to give it depth, and dangled dark gemstones from its edges. Adding even more decadence, lengths of silk ribbon replace a chain, allowing you to wear it as a short choker or as an opera-length piece.

Materials

set of US 0000 (1.25mm) straight knitting needles

30-gauge Argentium or sterling silver soft round wire (about 18' [549cm]) cut into a 10' (305cm) piece, a 6' (183cm) piece and a 2' (61cm) piece for sewing

2 21-gauge Argentium or sterling silver jump rings, soldered closed (5mm [.2"])

$\frac{7}{20}$" (9mm) wide silk ribbon (black is shown), enough to fit around your neck and tie (38" [97cm] as shown here, cut into 2 19" [48cm] lengths)

about 3" × 2" (7.6cm × 5cm) silk velvet (black is shown)

1 smoky quartz pear-cut flat briolette (or equivalent), about 4mm × 7.5mm ($\frac{5}{32}$" × $\frac{3}{10}$"), top-drilled

2 smoky quartz smooth teardrops (or equivalent) about 4.5mm × 9mm ($\frac{9}{50}$" × $\frac{7}{20}$"), top-drilled

4 garnet pear-cut briolettes (or equivalent) about 6mm × 4mm ($\frac{15}{64}$" × $\frac{5}{32}$"), top-drilled

nylon-covered coiling flat-jaw pliers (if making your own findings)

wire cutters

clear epoxy or jeweler's cement

clear nail polish

toothpick or pin (for placement of epoxy)

jeweler's tweezers

scissors

Pattern

Cast on 10 sts with the 10' (305cm) piece of wire.

Row 1: K10.

Row 2: P10.

Row 3: Kfb, k9 = 11.

Row 4: P11.

Row 5: Kfb, k9, kfb = 13.

Row 6: P13.

Row 7: Kfb, k11, kfb = 15.

Row 8: Add jump ring between the first two stitches and then p4, add new wire (the 6' [183cm] piece) (W2), BO1 with W2, p10 = 14.

Row 9: K10 with Wire 2 (W2); k4 with Wire 1 (W1).

Row 10: P4 with W1; p2tog, p8 with W2 = 13.

Row 11: K2tog, k5, k2tog with W2; k2tog, k2 with W1 = 10.

Row 12: P3 with W1; p2tog, p5 with W2 = 9.

Row 13: Kfb, k3, k2tog with W2; kfb, k2 with W1 = 10.

Row 14: P2tog, p2 with W1; p2tog, p4 with W2 = 8.

Row 15: K5 with W2; kfb, k2 with W1 = 9.

Row 16: P4 with W1; p2tog, p3 with W2 = 8.

Row 17: K4 with W2; kfb, k3 with W1 = 9.

Row 18: P5 with W1; p4 with W2 = 9.

Row 19: K4 with W2; kfb, k4 with W1 = 10.

Row 20: P6 with W1; p4 with W2 = 10.

Row 21: Kfb, k3 with W2; kfb, k5 with W1 = 12.

Row 22: P7 with W1; p2tog, p3 with W2 = 11.

Row 23: K4 with W2; k7 with W1 = 11.

Row 24: P2tog, p5 with W1; p4 with W2 = 10.

Row 25: K3, kfb with W2; k6 with W1 = 11.

Row 26: P4, p2tog with W1; p5 with W2 = 10.

Row 27: K2tog, k2, kfb with W2; k5 with W1 = 10.

Row 28: P5 with W1; p5 with W2 = 10.

Row 29: K2tog, k2, kfb with W2; kfb, k4 with W1 = 11.

Row 30: P6 with W1; p5 with W2 = 11.

Row 31: K4, kfb with W2; kfb, k5 with W1 = 13.

Row 32: P7 with W1; p6 with W2 = 13.

Row 33: Kfb, k4, kfb with W2; kfb, k6 with W1 = 16.

Row 34: P2tog, p14 with W1, leaving behind W2 (do not cut off the remaining wire) = 15.

Row 35: K15.

Row 36: Add jump ring between the first 2 stitches then p13, p2tog = 14.

Row 37: K2tog, k12 = 13.

Row 38: P2tog, p11 = 12.

Row 39: K2tog, k10 = 11.

Row 40: P2tog, p9 = 10.

Row 41: K2tog, k8 = 9.

Row 42: P2tog, BO2, p5 = 6.

Row 43: K2tog 3 times = 3.

Bind off.

Do not cut the extra wire. Instead use it to wrap the perimeter of the piece, taking care to wrap through the jump rings. Use the remaining dropped wire to wrap the created gap. Cut both wires close to the wire wraps and tuck ends in with tweezers. Place a drop of epoxy at each end to secure.

Assemble Necklace

Hold the velvet piece (tufted side up) under the knit piece (knit side up) covering the gap. Cut 18" (46cm) from the remains of wire 2 for the sewing of the velvet to the silver. Although in this project only the perimeter of the inner cavity will be sewn, please refer to *Green Ribbon Cuff* (page 96) for further instruction on this technique. Once the velvet has been sewn, use scissors to cut it as close to the gap edge as possible so the velvet doesn't show through the surrounding stitches.

Cut both ends of the ribbons into decorative *V* shapes. Coat the edges lightly with a bit of clear nail polish to keep them from fraying. Tie 1 end of each of the ribbons to each of the jump rings tightly, effectively turning the piece on its side, so that now the left side with the rings is the top, with the knit side facing you.

Cut 7 pieces from the remaining wire measuring 1" (2.5cm) each and thread each through a different bead. After the wire has gone through the drilled holes in the beads about halfway, cross the two ends over each other and twist, securing the bead and trimming the wire (as outlined on page 33).

Thread the flat smoky quartz briolette through the first stitch on the 22nd row (count along the bottom edge from left to right as the knit side faces you and the top edge has the ribbons attached). Cross the threaded wire over the twist and wrap to secure.

In the same manner, thread the 2 smoky quartz smooth teardrops, the first through the 11th row, and the second at the first stitch of the 33rd row, still counting from left to right. Finally, attach each of the 4 remaining garnet teardrops with a loop, again counting from left to right; the first at the 5th row, the second at the 17th row, the third at the 29th row and the fourth at the 39th row. Because each piece will be unique, it may be necessary to move the beads to another stitch in order to keep them balanced around the center flat smoky quartz briolette.

VIKING NECKLACE

Materials

28-gauge soft round sterling silver or silver-colored copper wire (about 40½' [1234cm])

2 pieces of 1.75mm (.07") round cable chain (each about 2½" [6.4cm] long)

2 pieces of 1.75mm (.07") round cable chain (each about 6" [15cm])

3 23-gauge Argentium or sterling silver jump rings soldered closed (4mm [.16"]) (or make your own from 23-gauge wire)

23-gauge Argentium or sterling silver hook clasp, about ⁵⁄₁₆" × ⁹⁄₅₀" (8mm × 4.5mm) (or make your own to similar dimensions using 23-gauge wire)

nylon-covered coiling flat-jaw pliers (if making your own findings)

small C-clamp

vise grip

wooden drawplate

needle- or round-nose pliers

wire cutters

clear epoxy or jeweler's cement

toothpick or pin (for placement of epoxy)

jeweler's tweezers

⁵⁄₃₂" (4mm) hexagonal wrench

a few pieces of scrap wire

Polished and classic, these two strands of Viking knitting are looped together to form one long, draping piece. The slinky cords are actually knit into two different lengths and attached as two separate necklaces.

Pattern

See pages 24–27 for more on the Viking knitting technique.

For Upper Cord:

Cut about 17' (518cm) of wire.

Cast on 7 sts, as outlined on page 24; mark 1st loop.

Viking knit 61 rows using the 5⁄32" (4mm) hex wrench.

Bind off.

Tie a scrap piece of string or wire to the flower end of the piece in progress and twist it together with the rest of the ends and the marker wire. Remove the piece in progress from the wrench. Thread the twisted end through the 1⁄8" (3.2mm) hole in the drawplate and firmly but gently pull the work through.

For Lower Cord:

Cut about 23' (701cm) of wire.

Cast on 7 sts as outlined on page 24; mark 1st loop.

Viking knit 97 rows using the 5⁄32" (4mm) hex wrench.

Bind off.

Tie a scrap piece of string or wire to the flower end of the piece in progress and twist it together with the rest of the ends and the marker wire. Remove the piece in progress from the wrench. Thread the twisted end through the 1⁄8" (3.2mm) hole in the drawplate and firmly but gently pull the work through.

Assemble Necklace

Once the 2 cords are finished, remove the flower-petal loops made at the beginning of each cord. Cut the remaining wire back to about 2" (5cm) so that it is easier to handle and thread it through the loops that have just been exposed. Once all the loops have been threaded, pull the wire tight to close the tube. This will now be the first part of a wrapped loop. Repeat with the other cord.

Thread the wire of the shorter cord through the end link of one of the 6" (15cm) pieces of chain. Cross the wire over the link and over itself and wrap the wire around itself (as outlined on page 33). Cut it close to the wrap and tuck in with tweezers. Place a drop of epoxy to seal.

Cut 2 lengths of the silver wire to about 2" (5cm) each. At the other, bound-off end of the shorter cord, thread 1 of them halfway through any 2 opposing stitches and then continue to thread into the others, working in opposite directions, ending at the opposite side. Pull both ends of the wire to close the tube and twist together. Clip one of the wire ends and thread the other through an end link of the other 6" (15cm) piece of chain. Wrap a loop. The shorter cord should now have a 6" (15cm) piece of chain attached to each end.

Repeat the above process to attach both 2½" (6.4cm) pieces of chain to either end of the larger cord.

Once the chains have been attached to the larger cord, take 2 1" (2.5cm) pieces of wire and thread each wire through the loose end link of a different chain. With a wrapped loop, attach the chains to the loops connecting the smaller cord to the long chains, as shown at left.

Finally, attach the clasp and jump ring with 2 more loops to the end links of the 2 long chains. Because there is no wrong side to this necklace, sides do not matter.

113

Although it may look complicated, this shape is made up of a basic square Stockinette panel. Once it's knit and wrapped, the square is rolled into a cone and stitched with wire to secure the shape. Beads are then wrapped together and tied on the inside as dangles. Juicy carnelian beads looped onto lengths of chain are added to form decorative drapes.

LILY NECKLACE

Materials

set of US 0000 (1.25mm) straight knitting needles

30-gauge Argentium or sterling silver soft round wire, about 18' (549cm) for knitting and wrapping and another 2' (61cm) for adding beads, etc.

3 lengths of 1.75mm (.07") round cable chain, one about 17½" (44cm) and the other 2 each about 1½" (4cm)

23-gauge Argentium or sterling silver jump ring soldered closed (4mm [.16"]) (or make your own from 23-gauge wire)

23-gauge Argentium or sterling silver hook clasp about ⁵⁄₁₆" × ⁹⁄₅₀" (8mm × 4.5mm) (or you can make your own to similar dimensions using 23-gauge wire)

13 carnelian smooth teardrop beads (or equivalent) about 4.5mm × 9mm (⁹⁄₅₀" × ⁷⁄₂₀"), top-drilled

nylon-covered coiling flat-jaw pliers (if making your own findings)

wire cutters

clear epoxy or jeweler's cement

toothpick or pin (for placement of epoxy)

jeweler's tweezers

Pattern

Cast on 22 sts.

Rows 1, 3, 5, 7, 9, 11, 13, 15, 17, 19, 21, 23 and 25: K22.

Rows 2, 4, 6, 8, 10, 12, 14, 16, 18, 20, 22 and 24: P22.

Bind off and then use the tweezers to squeeze together and then straighten the bound-off stitches (as outlined on page 23). Do not cut off extra wire. Pull the side edges of the knit piece to even out the stitches and then use the extra wire to begin wrapping the perimeter of the knitted piece (as outlined on page 28). After the whole piece has been wrapped, cut the wire close to the edges, tuck the end into the wrapping and seal with a bead of epoxy.

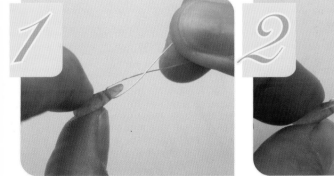

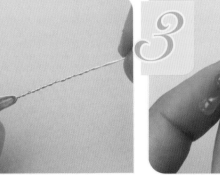

Assemble Necklace

Cut 3 lengths of 30-gauge wire to a length of about 6" (15cm). Thread a bead onto the center of each one and fold the wire ends together (**Figure 1**, page 115). Begin to twist them to secure the bead in place (**Figure 2**, page 115). Continue twisting all the way to the ends where they meet. Repeat for the other 2 lengths of wire.

Hold the beads together to form a cluster of drops and twist their wires together all the way to the ends (**Figure 3**, page 115).

Take the knitted and wrapped wire piece and, with the knit side on the outside, fold 2 diagonal corners in toward each other (**Figure 4**). Use your fingers to work the piece into a lily shape, joining the 2 corners, laying the right one over the left one (**Figure 5**).

Lay the twisted wire inside the lily, holding the beads inside the knitted piece and arrange it so the beads are just barely peeking out of the larger end of the lily shape (**Figure 6**). Bend the wire down over the knitting just to temporarily hold everything in place.

Cut a length of about 12" (30cm) of wire, make sure one edge of the knitted lily piece is slightly overlapping the other, and thread the wire through the bottom loop of both overlapping pieces (**Figure 7**). Pull it through almost all the way and bend the wire end to hold it temporarily in place (**Figure 8**).

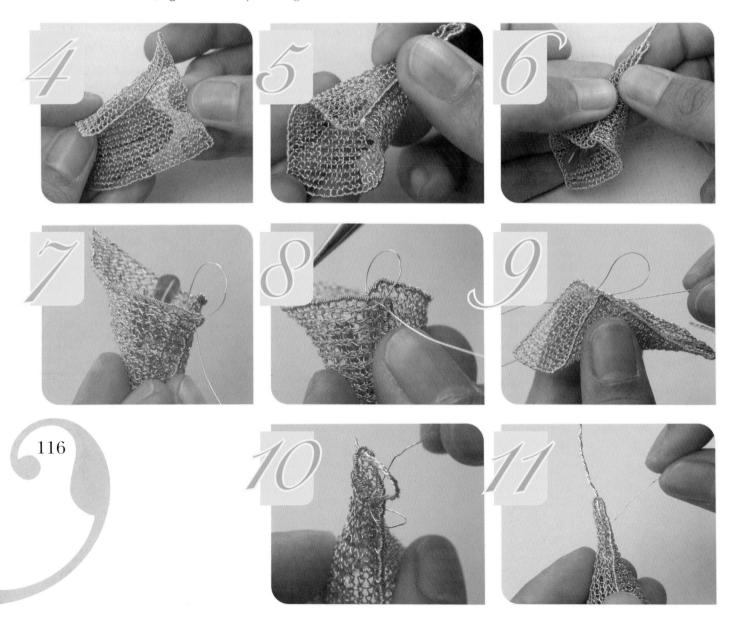

Slowly begin whipstitching along the edge of the top fold of the lily shape to secure it closed (**Figure 9**). Your stitches should be concealed in the wire wrapping. When you reach the other end of the piece, lift the tucked-in twisted wire ends away from the work. As you make the final stitch, take it behind these wire ends to secure them to the piece (**Figure 10**).

Tighten the stitch and then pull the twisted wire ends at the top into the position you want so the beads dangle properly. Continue to whipstitch around this top portion to secure it as much as you can—it will be tight (**Figure 11**). When you're done, trim the working wire and tuck in the end with tweezers or pliers. Do the same to the wire end at the bottom of the piece.

Use your fingers to form the piece so it's not quite so stiff and square. Use wire cutters to cut the wire twist about ⅛" (3.2mm) from the top of the piece (**Figure 12**). Splay out the ends of the wires and use tweezers to carefully tuck each one into the top of the piece (**Figure 13**).

Wrap complete loops (as outlined on page 33) through 4 of the carnelian beads (**Figure 14**). Now make a loop by threading a short length of wire through the topmost loop of the knitted piece, twisting it a few times and threading 2 of the knotted beads onto the wire (**Figure 15**).

Thread the wire through a loop in the center of the longest piece of chain (about 8¾" [22cm] from each end), and thread on 2 more beads to create a symmetrical dangle (**Figure 16**). Bring the loose end of the wire back together with the end attached to the lily and twist the wire closed. Trim the excess and tuck in the end.

Tie 1 of the carnelian beads to each end link of the 2 short lengths of chain, using wrapped loops, and another to the middle link of each chain. Measure 1" (2.5cm) to the right of the center link of the long chain, holding the lily with its beads facing you (about 18 links). Using a wrapped loop, attach an end of one of the small chains with beads. Making sure the beads are dangling toward the bottom, once more tie a loop to attach the smaller chain 1" (2.5cm) to the right (2" [5cm] from the center) (**Figure 17**). Repeat the process, but this time to the left of the lily.

Finally, use 2 more wrapped loops to attach the clasp on the left chain (with the lily's beads facing you) and the jump ring to the right side.

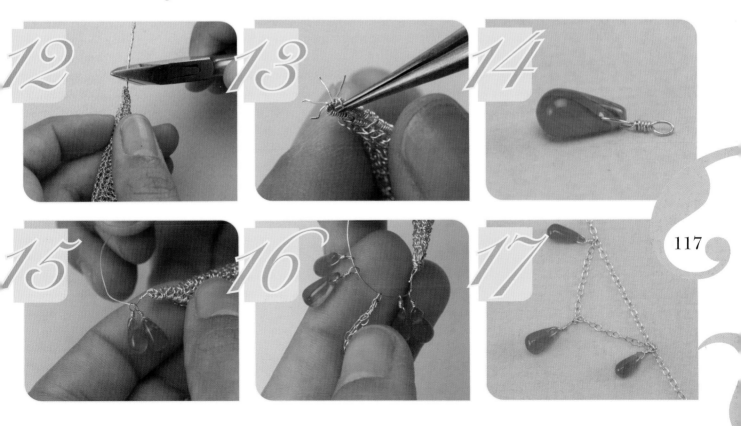

The shape of this oversize teardrop is amplified by knitting in small turquoise chips in descending numbers as you knit from the bottom up. You can mimic the gravity of the shape by clustering large numbers of pebbles in the wide bottom and more sparingly at the top. Clustered together, the different shades of turquoise create a rich texture. This piece goes to show that a large number of small, inexpensive gemstones can combine to form a bold, elegant piece.

TURQUOISE NECKLACE

Pattern

Cast on 10 sts.

Row 1: Kfb, k8, kfb = 12.

Row 2: P12, randomly adding 3 beads.

Row 3: Kfb, k10, kfb = 14.

Row 4: P14, randomly adding 4 beads.

Row 5: Kfb, k12, kfb = 16.

Row 6: P16, randomly adding 5 beads.

Row 7: K16.

Row 8: P2tog, p14, randomly adding 6 beads = 15.

Row 9: K2tog, k13 = 14.

Row 10: P2tog, p12, randomly adding 5 beads = 13.

Row 11: K2tog, k11 = 12.

Row 12: P12, randomly adding 3 beads.

Row 13: K12.

Row 14: P2tog, p10, randomly adding 3 beads = 11.

Row 15: K2tog, k9 = 10.

Row 16: P10, randomly adding 2 beads.

Row 17: K10.

Row 18: P10, randomly adding 2 beads.

Row 19: K2tog, k8 = 9.

Row 20: P2tog, p7 = 8.

Row 21: K8.

Row 22: P8, randomly adding 1 bead.

Row 23: K2tog, k4, k2tog = 6.

Row 24: P6, randomly adding 1 bead.

Row 25: K6.

Row 26: P6.

Row 27: K2tog, k2, k2tog = 4.

Row 28: P4, randomly adding 1 bead.

Row 29: K4.

Row 30: P4.

Row 31: [K2tog] twice.

Row 32: P2tog.

Bind off while adding the 5mm (.2") jump ring, if soldered closed (similar to the technique for adding an ear wire, illustrated on page 31).

Do not cut the excess wire. Instead use it to wrap the perimeter, making sure you wrap through the jump ring, if soldered closed. Trim the wire close to the wraps, tuck in the end with a pair of tweezers and secure with a drop of epoxy.

Materials

set of US 0000 (1.25mm) straight knitting needles

30-gauge Argentium or sterling silver soft round wire (about 18' [549cm]) for knitting and wrapping

21-gauge Argentium or sterling silver jump ring, soldered closed (5mm [.2"]) (or make your own out of 18-gauge wire, making sure the outer diameter is 5mm [.2"])

23-gauge Argentium or sterling silver jump ring, soldered closed (4mm [.16"]) (or make your own from 23-gauge wire)

23-gauge Argentium or sterling silver hook clasp, about 8mm × 4.5mm ($\frac{5}{16}$" × $\frac{9}{50}$") (or make your own to similar dimensions using 23-gauge wire)

1.75mm (.07") round cable chain about 17" (43cm) long

36 6mm–7mm ($\frac{15}{64}$"–$\frac{7}{25}$") turquoise chips, center-drilled

nylon-covered coiling flat-jaw pliers (if making your own findings)

needle- or round-nose pliers

wire cutters

clear epoxy or jeweler's cement

toothpick or pin (for placement of epoxy)

jeweler's tweezers

Assemble Necklace

Using a 1" (2.5cm) piece of 30-gauge wire, attach the 4mm (.16") jump ring to one end of the chain with a wrapped loop (see page 33). Thread the other end of the chain through the jump ring at the top of the pendant and repeat wrapping a loop at the other end of the chain in order to secure the clasp.

119

Although I collect specimens of them, I have never been fond of butterflies outside of the realm of science. In the commercial world, representations of butterflies seem always to show them not as real insects but rather as little girls' glittery keepsakes. However, by constructing my butterfly in sections—knit from different patterns and then sewn together—I gave it a more three-dimensional, realistic feel than other butterfly jewelry. The sparkling smoky quartz beads that serve as the butterfly's body only hint at its commercial fate as a child's jewelled trinket.

BUTTERFLY PENDANT

Materials

set of US 0000 (1.25mm) straight knitting needles

5 pieces 30-gauge Argentium or sterling silver soft round wire cut to the following lengths: 2 48" (122cm) lengths for the top wings, 2 36" (91cm) lengths for the bottom wings, and a 24" (61cm) remaining piece for beading, sewing, etc.

3 23-gauge Argentium or sterling silver jump rings, soldered closed (4mm [.16"]) (or make your own from 23-gauge wire)

23-gauge Argentium or sterling silver hook clasp, about ⁵⁄₁₆" × ⁹⁄₅₀" (8mm × 4.5mm) (or make your own to similar dimensions using 23-gauge wire)

2 9" (23cm) lengths of 1mm (.04") round cable chain

5 round beads 4mm (⁵⁄₃₂"), smoky quartz (or similar)

nylon-covered coiling flat-jaw pliers (if making your own findings)

needle- or round-nose pliers

wire cutters

clear epoxy or jeweler's cement

toothpick or pin (for placement of epoxy)

jeweler's tweezers

Pattern

Right Top Wing:

Cast on 4 sts.

Row 1: K4.

Row 2: P4.

Row 3: K3, kfb = 5.

Row 4: P5.

Row 5: K5.

Row 6: P5.

Row 7: K4, kfb = 6.

Row 8: P6.

Row 9: Kfb, k5 = 7.

Row 10: P7.

Row 11: Kfb, k5 kfb = 9.

Row 12: P7, p2tog = 8.

Row 13: K8.

Row 14: P6, p2tog = 7.

Row 15: BO3 sts, k4 = 4.

Row 16: P2, p2tog.

Add the jump ring while binding off. Do not cut excess wire.

Left Top Wing:

Cast on 4 sts.

Row 1: K4.

Row 2: P4.

Row 4: Kfb, k3 = 5.

Row 5: P5.

Row 6: K5.

Row 7: P5.

Row 8: Kfb, k4 = 6.

Row 9: P6.

Row 10: K5, kfb = 7.

Row 11: P7.

Row 12: Kfb, k5, kfb = 9.

Row 13: P2tog, p7 = 8.

Row 14: K6, k2tog = 7.

Row 15: BO2, k5 = 5.

Row 16: K3, k2tog = 4.

Row 17: P2tog, p2 = 3.

Add a jump ring while binding off. Do not cut excess wire.

Right Bottom Wing:

Cast on 5 sts.

Row 1: K5.

Row 2: P5.

Row 3: Kfb, k4 = 6.

Row 4: P6.

Row 5: K6.

Row 6: P6.

Row 7: Kfb, k5 = 7.

Row 8: P2tog, p5 = 6.

Row 9: Kfb, k5 = 7.

Bind off.

Do not cut excess wire.

Left Bottom Wing:

Cast on 5 sts.

Row 1: K5.

Row 2: P5.

Row 3: K4, kfb = 6.

Row 4: P6.

Row 5: K6.

Row 6: P6.

Row 7: K5, kfb = 7.

Row 8: P5, P2tog = 6.

Row 9: K5, kfb = 7.

Bind off.

Do not cut excess wire.

Wrap all 4 pieces with their leftover wires, making sure to wrap through the jump rings on the top wings. Cut the wires flush to the wraps, tuck in the ends with tweezers and secure with epoxy beads.

Assemble Necklace

With the knit sides facing up, place the cast-on rows of the 2 bottom wings together (the stitches should now be running sideways away from each other). Cut a 4" (10cm) piece of wire and thread 1 end up through the first stitch at the bottom left corner of the right bottom wing. Leave a ½" (1cm) tail at the bottom and bend to secure temporarily. Pass the wire to the left over both cast-on edges and down through the bottom right stitch of the left bottom wing. Sew the wire under the cast-on edges toward the right and up through the next stitch up (from the first one sewn) on the bottom right wing. Now pass it over the edges again to the left and into the opposing stitch on the bottom left wing. Continue in this manner until all 5 cast-on stitches on both sides have been sewn together. Repeat the sewing process for the 2 top wings, making sure they are knit side up.

Once both sets of wings have been sewn, place the top set slightly over the bottom 2 (so the bottom stitches of the top wings are directly over the top stitches of the bottom wings), making sure the cast-on rows match up in the middle. Cut another 4" (10cm) piece of wire and thread 1 end up through the bottom left stitch on the bottom right wing, leaving a ½" (1cm) tail. Straddle the cast-on row by threading the tail up through the bottom right stitch of the bottom left wing. Both ends should now be opposite each other on the knit side. Tie a simple knot (make a loop by crossing them and then passing one end through the loop and tighten) and then press the 2 ends together.

Thread the beads with the longer wire, but make sure the shorter end goes into the drilled hole of the first bead; the first bead should be threaded by 2 wires. Now pull the wire up to the top center edge along the cast-on rows and thread the wire over the edge and then up through the top left stitch of the top right wing. Sew the wire over the center down through the top right stitch of the top left wing. Repeat the sewing, but this time skip down 2 stitches (or equivalent) to the opening between the 2 first beads (in this case, it was the third stitch down from the top) and sew across, effectively clamping down the wire going through the beads. Continue sewing around the center stitches and over the bead wire until all 5 beads have been secured, as shown. Thread the wire down and around the bottom cast-on rows and then wrap tightly around the bottom 2 beads. Cut the wire close and tuck in with tweezers. Place a drop of epoxy with a toothpick to secure.

Using the wrapped loop technique, attach 1 end of one of the chain lengths to one of the jump rings on the top wings. Repeat with the second chain for the other wing. Attach the remaining jump ring to the last link of the chain on the right side and the clasp to the left side with 2 more wrapped loops (reverse sides if you are left-handed). Tuck in the loose ends and secure with additional drops of epoxy.

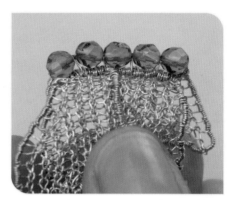

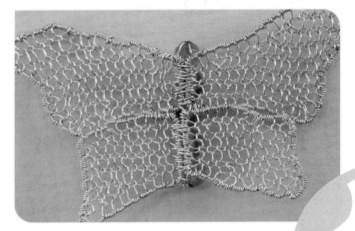

Gallery

Most of the supplies used in this book can be found at your local craft, bead, art, jewelry and even hardware stores. But if you have difficulties obtaining any of the supplies locally, the list of vendors below might be of some help.

RESOURCES

Angelika's Yarn Store

www.yarn-store.com

Size 0000 double-pointed knitting needles

Artistic Wire Ltd.

www.artisticwire.com

Colored copper wire

Dick Blick Art Materials

www.dickblick.com

Jewelry supplies, burnisher

Fire Mountain Gems and Beads

www.firemountaingems.com

Wire, beads, chain and findings, rubber cord, jewelry-making tools, adhesives

JewelrySupply.com

www.jewelrysupply.com

Wire, sheet metal, chain and findings, rubber cord, beads, jewelry-making tools, adhesives, patina supplies, polishing supplies

Metalliferous

www.metalliferous.com

Wire, sheet metal, chain and findings, jewelry-making tools, adhesives, patina supplies, polishing supplies

M&J Trimming

www.mjtrim.com

Ribbons, trimmings

Rio Grande

www.riogrande.com

Beads, wire, sheet metal, rubber cord, jewelry-making tools, adhesives, patina supplies, polishing supplies

Brown & Sharpe Wire Gauge Chart

Gauge	Inches	mm
0	.325	8.26
2	.257	6.54
4	.204	5.19
6	.162	4.12
8	.128	3.26
10	.102	2.59
12	.081	2.05
13	.072	1.83
14	.064	1.63
15	.057	1.45
16	.051	1.29
18	.040	1.02
19	.036	.912
20	.032	.812
21	.028	.723
22	.025	.644
23	.023	.573
24	.020	.511
25	.018	.455
26	.016	.405
27	.014	.360
28	.013	.321
29	.011	.286
30	.010	.255
32	.0080	.2019
34	.0063	.1600

INDEX

INDULGE YOUR CREATIVE SIDE WITH THESE OTHER F+W MEDIA TITLES

ISBN-10: 1-58180-650-7
ISBN-13: 978-1-58180-650-2
paperback, 128 pages, #33239

Bead on a Wire
SHARILYN MILLER

In her latest book, magazine editor and popular author Sharilyn Miller shows crafters of all levels how to get in on the popularity of jewelry and beading. Inside *Bead on a Wire*, you'll find an in-depth section on design and construction techniques that make it a snap to get started. You'll love to make the 20 step-by-step bead and wire jewelry projects, including gorgeous earrings, necklaces, brooches and bracelets. You'll be amazed at how easy it is to start making fashionable jewelry that's guaranteed to inspire compliments.

ISBN-10: 1-60061-159-1
ISBN-13: 978-1-60061-159-9
paperback with flaps, 144 pages, #Z2508

Bead and Wire Jewelry Exposed
MARGOT POTTER, KATIE HACKER & FERNANDO DASILVA

Bead & Wire Jewelry Exposed features over 50 high-fashion jewelry pieces made using techniques that reveal typically hidden components. Beading wire, cording, findings, tubing and chain take center stage in these clever designs. You'll learn to make shiny metallic wire or jump rings the focus of a design, and you'll see that a clasp can be decorative as well as functional. While the pieces may look complex, the techniques are simple enough for beginners—yet the designs are sophisticated enough for veteran jewelry crafters. Each of the three authors, Margot Potter, Katie Hacker and Fernando DiSilva, puts his or her spin on the exposed-element designs, so there's something for everyone.

ISBN-10: 1-58180-646-9
ISBN-13: 978-1-58180-646-5
paperback, 128 pages, #33235

Metal Craft Discovery Workshop
LINDA & OPIE O'BRIEN

Discover a nontraditional approach to the introduction of working with metal as you create 20 fun and funky projects. This is the whimsical side of metal that not only teaches you how to cut and join metal surfaces, but also allows you to explore ways to age and add texture to metal, conjure up beautiful patina finishes and uncover numerous types of metal such as copper, mesh, wire and recycled material. Whether you've worked with metal before or you're new to the medium, give your recyled tin cans a second glance and start crafting beautiful pieces with metal today.